SEE EE LIFE THROUGH ROSE-COLORED GLASSES

ROBYN BARNHARDT

Charleston, SC
www.PalmettoPublishing.com

See Life Through Rose-Colored Glasses
Copyright © 2022 by Robyn Barnhardt

First Edition

Hardcover: 979-8-88590-261-8
Paperback: 979-8-88590-262-5
eBook: 979-8-88590-263-2

For MacDaddy:
Without your Yang *to my* Yin, *I never would*
have gone looking for something more.

Table of Contents

Introduction

Don't let the title fool you. This isn't a feel-good, "don't worry be happy" kind of book. Well, it sort of is, but it is so much more than that. This is a how-to, a tutorial, an instruction book on how to see things differently—how to change patterns of thought and learn to focus in a way that gives you more control over your life.

Life is not just happening to you. You're the boss. You are in the driver's seat, and you have a lot more control over where you're going than you think you do. But how? How do you actually go about it? How do you get from where you are to where you want to be?

Years ago, I saw an interview with a young woman named Rudine Howard on *The Oprah Winfrey Show*. Rudine suffered from anorexia nervosa, and at the time of the interview, she was twenty-nine years old and weighed only fifty-eight pounds. She was a prisoner trapped in a malnourished and frail body. She was starving to death; not just physically but mentally and spiritually as well. She couldn't see a way out. She wanted to die.

Tracey Gold, an actress who had also battled anorexia, was another guest on the show. Though she had once been in Rudine's shoes, she had successfully fought the disease and had come out the other side. Sitting next to Rudine on the stage, Tracey struggled to help Rudine understand that there was hope. By taking baby steps, making small changes, and putting one foot in front of the other, she too could choose to live a different life. It was a choice.

I still remember Rudine listening intently to Tracey's every word with tears in her eyes, asking, "But *how* do you do it?" She clearly wanted with all of her heart to break out of the prison she had created for herself, but she didn't know where to begin. The presence or absence of food was not what was killing Rudine, but how she chose to think about food and what it represented. She had been battling anorexia for seventeen years, and though her thoughts and beliefs about food were killing her, she didn't know how to let them go and trust another way of thinking. She couldn't see the baby steps. She could only see an insurmountable mountain. Rudine died of anorexia in 1996 at the age of thirty-one.

This is an extreme example of destructive thought patterns, but the premise is true for all of us. Your thoughts are either taking you closer to where you want to be, or they're taking you in the opposite direction. This is easy to understand intellectually, but just like Rudine wanted to know, exactly *how* do you do it? How do you change your detrimental patterns of thoughts to ones that are more beneficial? How do you take the baby steps to turn them around?

In order to explain what I have learned about this, I'm going to use the metaphor of putting on "rose-colored glasses" to illustrate the art of choosing a more intentional perspective. This isn't about being in denial. This is about being mindful of where you are and deliberately focusing on what you want and how you want to feel. What you are choosing to see and believe—and it is a choice—whether you are doing it intentionally or by default is paramount in determining the quality of the life you are living.

I took a visual arts class in college. Before we began to paint, the instructor taught us that learning to paint started with training your eye to actually *see* the subject. She told us to stop trying to draw the subject the way we thought it *should* look or paint it the color we assumed it *should* be, but to step back, squint our eyes, and analyze what we were actually seeing. Then, and only then, could we realistically translate it to the canvas.

She was giving us a lesson in perspective. Water may appear blue when it's reflecting back a bright blue sky, but if the sky is cloudy, the water may appear gray or even black. The farther away a subject is, the smaller and more muted it will appear. Just like you can train your eyes to look for obscure details to paint, you can learn to change the quality of your thoughts with deliberate focus and mindfully decide what you choose to perceive.

When you have no control over your thoughts, life can feel like you are in the back seat of a car being driven by a maniac. You feel like you are holding on for dear life, out of control, at the mercy of chance and circumstance. It's not a good feeling. But you don't have to live life from that defensive, helpless point of view.

Let's take this step-by-step. Instead of our reactionary thoughts running the show, we are going to choose the thoughts we want to entertain. We are going to reevaluate and fine-tune our perspective. We're going to consciously pay attention to our thoughts and emotions and understand what they mean. And then from this calm, relaxed state, we are going to get control of this thing. We're going to get in the driver's seat, adjust our mirrors, and purposely drive in the direction we want to go. And what's more—we're going to enjoy the ride.

"SHE KNEW *the power* OF HER MIND AND SO PROGRAMMED IT FOR SUCCESS."

CARRIE GREEN

12 Universal Laws:

Listed below are twelve principles that I will be referring to throughout the book. They are principles thought to be intrinsic, unchanging laws of the Universe. They consist of various philosophical perspectives, scientific laws, and theories that are based on an observed natural phenomenon or a unifying concept and refer to a precept or principle that is widely accepted as legitimate across locations, time periods, and cultures.

Law of Divine Oneness:
All things are connected. Everything is made up of Universal Energy coming from the same energetic source. (Hermetic Principle)

Law of Vibration:
Everything in the Universe is made up of energy and is in constant motion, vibrating at different frequencies. (Hermetic Principle, String Theory)

Law of Attraction:
The Universe is made up of energetic vibrations being drawn to other vibrations that are vibrating at the same frequency. Like energies attract. (Inspired by Hermeticism, Transcendentalism, Bible, Hinduism)

Law of Relativity:
Nothing (thought, person, emotion, action, etc.) can be evaluated or judged unless you can compare it in relation to something else. (Hermeticism)

Law of Polarity:
Everything exists in duality. For anything to exist at all, there has to be the potential for the absence of it. (Hermetic Principle)

Law of Perpetual Transmutation of Energy:
Everything in the Universe is evolving. There is no regression, only expansion. The Universe is constantly in a state of becoming more. (Based on Law of Conservation of Energy)

Law of Inspired Action:
Since everything is connected, this law refers to the ability to tap into the collective consciousness of all that is. The ability to receive inspiration for action, intuitively. (Panpsychism)

Law of Cause and Effect:
This law states that for every action, there is a reaction or impact. (Hermetic Principle)

Law of Correspondence:
Everything in the physical world has corresponding principles on all other planes. Light, vibration, and motion all have corresponding principles in the etheric plane. (Hermetic Principle)

Law of Compensation:
The Universe is both self-organizing and self-correcting. The natural order of the Universe is well-being. (Anthropic Principle)

Law of Rhythm:
The Universe has a precise rhythm similar to a pendulum that dictates the flow of energy, whereby it moves in and out, up and down, or left and right, suggesting that all Universal matter has a specific pattern or rhythm that it must follow for existence to emerge. (Hermetic Principle)

Law of Gender:
Everything has a masculine and feminine principle, which produces metaphysical forces that play a role in creation and regeneration. Everything in the Universe has a masculine and a feminine property. Everything *is* both masculine and feminine. (Hermetic Principle)

per·spec·tive
/pərˈspektiv/

noun

1. the art of drawing solid objects on a
    two-dimensional surface so as to give the right
    impression of their height, width, depth, and posi-
    tion in relation to each other when viewed from a
    particular point.
    "a perspective drawing"

2. a particular attitude toward or way of regarding
    something; a point of view.
    "most guidebook history is written from the editor's
    perspective"

NOWHERE
NOW HERE
It's just a matter of
perspective.
Choose your views wisely.
UNKNOWN

Perspective

Step 1—What Are You Looking At?

What do we want out of life? What is this pot of gold at the end of the rainbow that we are all chasing? If you were to take a poll asking people what they would ask for if they could have anything in the world, most would list things like: lots of money, a loving partner, good health, lavish vacations, a private jet, a yacht, power, fame, etc. Of course, right? But why? Why do we want those things? What does having those things do for you?

You want those things because you believe that having them in your possession will make you *feel* good. You want to *feel* happy. You want money so that you will *feel* secure. You want a satisfying relationship so that you will *feel* loved. You want power and fame so that you will *feel* important. You want to *feel* better. You want to *feel* at peace.

The only reason that we ever desire anything is that we believe the experience of having it will make us feel good. We want to be happy. That's the bottom-line motivation for anything you will ever want out of life.

Getting those kinds of things will make you feel good. It's exciting to get a new car or to go on a fantastic vacation. The elation of falling in love is unparalleled. Having your peers give you their attention and respect does feel validating. There is nothing wrong in wanting any of those things, and there is nothing wrong in getting them.

But having those things in your possession does not guarantee that you will feel happy. In fact, there are countless examples of powerful, wealthy people in the world who are miserable. That's why it can be so disillusioning to finally get things you want but still feel unfulfilled.

> *"I think everybody should get rich and do everything they ever dreamed of so they can see that it's not the answer."*
>
> —Jim Carrey

Getting the things we want is not the answer, but it's not the problem either. The problem is when you are dependent on things and other people to make you *feel* happy then you are going to be disappointed every time. There isn't a person alive or a possession you can own that has the ability to perpetuate your happiness over time. That's not how life works.

Although you can certainly have people and material things bring you the *feeling* of joy and happiness, the actual state of *being* happy is only based on your perception of it. It's never completely about them or the stuff.

That's why you can simultaneously have a multi-millionaire sitting on a private jet who is pissed off and miserable, and a single mom living paycheck-to-paycheck, who is ecstatic over

"Don't put your happiness in other people's hands. They'll drop it.

They'll drop it every time."

CHRISTOPHER BARZAK

getting a fifty-dollar tip. Whether it's fifty dollars or fifty million dollars, the monetary value is irrelevant to the thoughts and feelings they choose to have about it.

"The question is not what you look at, but what you see."

—Henry David Thoreau

Just like Rudine couldn't make the leap from delusional thinking about food to reclaiming her health in an instant, you can't adjust your perspective without understanding what it is and why you may need to change your focus.

Your personal perspective is how you see the world. It's the lens through which you choose to view your reality. It's the spin you use to evaluate what you see and determine what it means for you. Yes, we may all be living in the same world, looking at the same people, things, happenings, and events, but what we each choose to perceive creates a reality that is completely unique to us.

Have you ever been with an old friend or family member, reminiscing about something that happened years ago, and you both remember completely different versions of the same story? Why is that? Because whether you are remembering the past, visualizing the future, or observing the present moment, you are looking at it from your personal point of view—a point of view that has been shaped by your personal experiences and beliefs.

No two people in the world will have the same exact view because no two people have lived the same life. There's no such thing as an absolute true reality because we are all seeing it from a different angle.

It's like the parable of the blind men and the elephant:

A group of blind men heard that a strange animal called an elephant had been brought to the town, but none of them were aware of its shape and form. Out of curiosity, they said, "We must inspect it by touch." So, they sought it out and when they found it, began to grope about it. The first man whose hand was on the trunk said, "This animal is like a thick snake." Another, whose hand reached its ear said, "It seems like a kind of fan." Another man whose hand was on its leg said, "No, the elephant is like a pillar, like a tree trunk!" The blind man who placed his hand upon the elephant's side said, "It is a wall." Another felt its tail and described it as a rope. And the last man feeling its tusk said, "The elephant is hard and smooth—like a spear!"

Not one of them was wrong. The blind men were all correct from their own particular point of view. They were each focusing on the part of the elephant that was relevant to them.

"The moon is always full, it's just our view that is partial."

—Jackie Deakin

We've all been trained by others, and we have trained ourselves into specific patterns of thoughts. The way we're raised, the culture we grow up in, our relationships with our families, friends, and enemies, the books we read, the movies we watch, the music we listen to, etc.—everything in our experience has had an impact on our personal perspective. Our beliefs about ourselves, about others, and about the world around us determine how we *feel* about what we are observing.

Whether you are doing it consciously or subconsciously, you are using your observations and your personal beliefs to evaluate your surroundings at all times. You look at something and instantly make a judgment of good or bad, acceptable or unacceptable, pretty or ugly, etc. You are constantly critiquing, sizing up, and keeping score of everything in your field of vision. If you observe something that pleases you, you're happy. If you observe something that disappoints or upsets you, you're unhappy.

How do you know if your thoughts and beliefs are beneficial to you? How does most of what you observe in your life make you feel? Think about what you believe and why. I'm not necessarily just talking about religious or moral beliefs, but your general, observational beliefs as well. Maybe you believe things like:

- You'll never find true love.
- All the good ones are already married.
- There's a soulmate for everyone.

- All men are scumbags.
- What goes around comes around.
- Republicans are better than Democrats.
- Democrats are better than Republicans.
- Carbs are bad for you.
- If you don't go to church, you'll go to Hell.
- There's no such thing as Hell.
- There's no such thing as God.
- Rich people are greedy.
- Poor people are lazy.
- Children should be seen and not heard.
- Pets shouldn't be treated like children.
- Cats make better pets than dogs.
- Dogs are man's best friend.
- Technology is too advanced.
- Southerners are stupid.
- Yankees are rude.
- Etc., Etc., Etc.

For example, if you truly believe that all the good ones are married and you're never going to find true love, I don't care how many good ones are out there, you are never going to attract one. You are focused on what went wrong in every relationship you've ever been in. You are complaining about your exes and pointing out all of their shortcomings. Is it any wonder that you would continue to attract that same kind of dead-end relationship? You aren't even looking for anything else. And the fact that you continue to have that same kind of experience just reaffirms to you that your beliefs about love and marriage are true. It's like a vicious cycle of negativity.

Keep in mind that although there may be valid reasons for you to have the thoughts and beliefs that you have, it doesn't mean it's true in every instance. And even if it has been true in those past relationships, does it make you feel good to focus on the unwanted aspects of it? Why would you insist on dwelling on things that make you feel bad and are ultimately detrimental to your current state of mind?

If you are thinking thoughts that make you feel bad when you think them and then attracting a reality that you do not want, isn't it logical that it would be in your best interest to think thoughts that make you feel better? Maybe you should come at this from a different angle. There's more than one way to see an elephant, remember?

You can *choose* to focus on the negative aspects of a situation or you can *choose* to focus on the positive aspects. You may think a positive approach to life works when things are going well, but what happens when things are really difficult? It's easy to feel appreciation and be grateful when things are good, but what about when life throws you a curveball? Hardships and challenges are when your ability to alter your perspective matters most. This is when the power of reframing your view of a situation to better serve you, actually begins to "change" the situation.

Most people don't think too much about the thoughts they choose to entertain. In fact, most of us aren't "choosing" at all. We are just reacting to life and circumstances. This is what I call living life defensively. You observe and react. In order for you to *feel* happy, you have to observe what you believe will make you happy—conditions that are entirely out of your control. This can leave you feeling insecure, uncertain, and certainly not happy. You're letting a maniac drive

BAD NEWS IS:

You cannot make people like,
love, understand, validate,
accept or be nice to you.

GOOD NEWS IS:

It doesn't matter.

UNKNOWN

your car, so to speak.

You have to learn to shift your focus from outside factors that you have no control over to the only thing that you can control—you. You have absolute control over what you decide to give your attention to. Instead of reacting, you can choose to focus on a better-feeling thought. Taking total responsibility for how you feel and understanding the significance of that is monumental.

> *"You can't control how other people behave. You can't control everything that happens to you. What you can control is how you respond to it all. In your response is your power."*
>
> —Marc and Angel Chernoff

Your state of happiness is a direct result of what you choose to look for. Your life is as wonderful or as horrible as you allow it to be. If your state of mind is one of possibilities, growth, and optimism then that is what you will pay attention to and take notice of in your surroundings. If you choose to focus on scarcity, limited opportunities, and struggle, then those things will get your attention and become more apparent to you.

How often do you practice thoughts that bring you joy, comfort, and relief, and how often do you practice thoughts that make you anxious and full of fear and worry?

Just like my art instructor challenged her students to look at color, line, and perspective differently in order to paint, you can learn to fine-tune your focus to create purposeful, deliberate thoughts that bring you peace instead of anxiety. There are two sides to every coin. Two sides to every story. You get to choose. Instead of automatically assuming that the water is bright blue, let's look at it in a different light.

> *"From the moment I fell down that rabbit hole, I've been told where I must go and who I must be. But this is my dream. I'll decide where it goes from here."*
> —*Alice in Wonderland*

`re·al·ize

/ˈrē(ə)ˌlīz/

verb

1. to become fully aware of (something) as a fact; understand clearly.
   "he realized his mistake at once"

2. to cause (something desired or anticipated) to happen.
   "his worst fears have been realized"

"SHE REMEMBERED WHO SHE WAS AND THE GAME CHANGED."

LALAH DELIA

Realize

Step 2—Your Internal GPS System—Your Emotions

To really begin to shift your perspective, you must have an understanding of your emotions and what they are trying to tell you.

We all have an emotional guidance system. It's the inner part of us that is connected to the larger part of who we are. It's the spiritual part of our individual selves. Your emotional guidance system is how your soul communicates with your intellect. You've heard the phrase, "Let your conscience be your guide." It's the visceral, intuitive, and true knowing part of who you are.

> *"In science we call it energy. In religion we call it spirit. In the streets we call it vibes. All I'm saying is . . . trust it."*
>
> —Unknown

To break this down, we are going to step back and shift our focus to the panoramic view in order to take in the bigger picture—the bigger picture being Source, the Universe, God, etc. and your ability to tap into that.

Try not to get hung up on the terminology; this is not about challenging your theological beliefs and philosophies. The vocabulary you use is irrelevant. Water is water, whether you call it *agua (Spanish)*, *acqua (Italian)*, or *l'eau (French)*. If you get in it, you'll get wet—regardless of the language you choose. So going forward, I will refer to the bigger part of you as the Universe or Source and the individual part of you as your soul or spirit.

In the book *A Course in Miracles*, scribed by Helen Schucman, a medical psychology professor at Columbia University, she refers to enlightenment as a shift of the self-perception of self-identification—a shift from body identification to spirit identification. That is basically the understanding that you are a part of something bigger, and everything is connected energetically.

There's an analogy that Marianne Williamson used to explain this in an interview that was featured on *Oprah's Super Soul Conversations* that illustrates this perfectly. In the interview, she talks about accessing the part of us that is greater than our individual selves—how we all have the ability to *plug in* to the Universe, to *plug in* to a higher power.

She says, "Imagine the Universe is a big house that is wired for electricity, and we as individuals are all lamps. The lamps could be tall, short, any shape, any color, any design. The power of the lamp has to do with the electricity that allows the light to shine through it. No matter what the lamp looks like or how spectacular it is, if it's not plugged in, it doesn't shed any light. And the light isn't generated from the lamp but from the electricity. If we only think of ourselves as individuals, separate

"Learn how to see. Realize that everything connects to everything else."

LEONARDO DA VINCI

from the whole of who we are, then we are only identifying with the lamp—a dark vessel. If we identify with our spirit then we identify with something much bigger than us. The whole purpose of the lamp is to plug in so that the light shines through us. So that we self-actualize and become the lamp we were meant to be."

Don't you just love that?

> *"The lamps are different, but the light is the same."*
> —Rumi

So, let's visualize the Universe as this stream of incredible energy. A lightning-speed vibration of white light and unconditional love. It is all good things, all good feelings, and a sense of well-being that is infinite and inexhaustible, never ending. It's wired for electricity, and it is always available to you.

How do you access it? How can you tell when you are in tune with the larger part of who you are? You know you are plugged in, when your individual, emotional vibration has matched up with the higher vibrations of Source Energy. You know you are in the flow when you *feel* love, when you *feel* lightness and expansion, when you *feel* wholeness and joy. Your emotions and feelings are indicators of your vibrational frequency and your connection to Source.

> *"If you want to find the secrets of the Universe, think in terms of energy, frequency, and vibration."*
> —Nikola Tesla

In the past, scientific and spiritual theories may have been more antagonistic in nature, but science today acknowledges the historical, philosophical, and cultural links between science, the humanities, and spirituality. Most will agree that science alone cannot explain the mysteries of the Universe and that philosophy and spirituality must be included in any explanation of the unknown because it seems that one cannot exist without the other.

Quantum physics has proven that everything in the Universe is made up of energy. Every single thing, discernible to the human eye or not, is made up of vibrating energy. From light waves to sound waves to dense matter like rock and wood, even thoughts and feelings, are made up of millions and millions of subatomic particles of energy vibrating at different frequencies.

David R. Hawkins, M.D., PhD, is a renowned psychiatrist, physician, and spiritual teacher who is credited with developing the "Map of Consciousness." Using a technique called kinesiology, his studies and research show that our emotions are indicators of the frequency and vibration of our personal energy field at any given time. He developed a scoring system based on a logarithmic scale that spans from zero to 1000, with the highest numbers representing enlightenment or pure awareness.

His research is highly scientific and technical, but the takeaway is that the way you feel is indicative of where you stand vibrationally. And the rate at which you are vibrating is indicative of how plugged in you are. Our feelings and emotions serve as an important feedback system designed to help us understand our connection or disconnection from Source. Here is a chart representing the energy levels as he outlined them in relation to emotions:

Map of Consciousness
Developed by David R. Hawkins

The Map of Consciousness is based on a logarithmic
scale that spans from 1 to 1000

Name of Level	Energic Frequency	Associated Emotional State	View of Life
Enlightenment	700-1000	Ineffable	Is
Peace	600	Bliss	Perfect
Joy	540	Serenity	Complete
Love	500	Reverence	Benign
Reason	400	Understanding	Meaningful
Acceptance	350	Forgiveness	Harmonious
Willingness	310	Optimism	Hopeful
Neutrality	250	Trust	Satisfactory
Courage	200	Affirmation	Feasible
Pride	175	Scorn	Demanding
Anger	150	Hate	Antagonistic
Desire	125	Craving	Disappointing
Fear	100	Anxiety	Frightening
Grief	75	Regret	Tragic
Apathy	50	Despair	Hopeless
Guilt	30	Blame	Evil
Shame	20	Humiliation	Miserable

I also like this cone diagram of the same principle because it's a good illustration to represent the expansion or constriction of energy. As you vibrate at the lower end of the emotional scale you are literally contracting and cutting yourself off from Source. As you move up the scale to those better-feeling emotions, the energy expands, representing flow and connection.

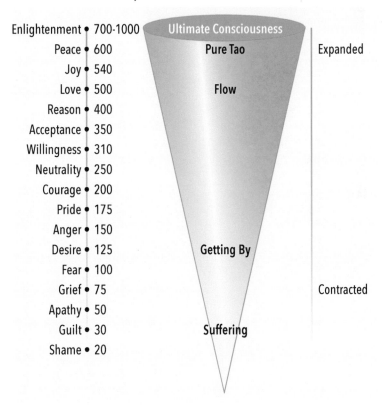

Cone Diagram of Map of Consciousness

Emotion	Value		Region
Enlightenment	700-1000	Ultimate Consciousness	
Peace	600	Pure Tao	Expanded
Joy	540		
Love	500	Flow	
Reason	400		
Acceptance	350		
Willingness	310		
Neutrality	250		
Courage	200		
Pride	175		
Anger	150		
Desire	125	Getting By	
Fear	100		
Grief	75		Contracted
Apathy	50		
Guilt	30	Suffering	
Shame	20		

"Everything is energy and that's all there is to it. Match the frequency of the reality you want and you cannot help but get that reality. It can be no other way.

This is not philosophy.
This is physics."

ALBERT EINSTEIN

The Law of Attraction states that vibrations of a similar frequency will draw together. Think of two droplets of water slowly moving towards each other. As they get closer to one another, they will merge into one large drop of water because they are vibrating at the same frequency. But a drop of water and a drop of oil will not merge because their vibrations are very different. It is the same with emotions and feelings.

You must become a vibrational match to whatever you desire in order to attract it into your reality. If you want love but are vibrating at the lower vibration of hate, you will not attract love into your reality. It doesn't matter how much you want it, how much you think you deserve it, or how much of it you think other people are getting—if you are not in the vibrational vicinity of it, you cannot manifest it. You don't get what you want; you get what you are.

Your personal vibration is the variable here. Source doesn't change to accommodate you. Source cannot be anything other than that lightning speed, white light of love and well-being. You have to raise your vibration to meet Source. When we look at ourselves, others, and situations negatively and differently from the way Source sees us, we experience the negative emotion of unplugging from the stream, unplugging from all that we are on a soul level. That is why it feels so uncomfortable. That negative emotion, that feeling of disconnection is your emotional guidance system kicking in. It's like the "check engine" light coming on in your car.

"The Universe doesn't speak English, it speaks frequency."

—Unknown

Do you know where you are vibrating on the emotional scale right now? Just because you verbalize the words "I'm fine" doesn't mean that is the way you actually feel. Feelings can be a complicated thing. Not only are they hard to label, but they can be almost impossible for us to recognize. There are literally thousands of words in the English language used to describe emotions. What's more is that you can feel multiple emotions at the same time, making it even more confusing.

You may think it's implausible that someone may not recognize what they are feeling but it is much more common than people realize. The main reason for this confusion is that we tend to intellectualize our emotions. We slap a label on them and disregard how we really feel. So, to navigate this, you have to get out of your head and into your gut. You have to disregard the language and feel your way through.

Take note of how you feel physically. How is your body reacting? Is your heart racing? Does your face and neck feel hot and splotchy? Are you super relaxed and at ease? Do you feel warm and fuzzy? Do you have butterflies in your stomach? Do the butterflies make you feel excited or make you feel like you're going to throw up? Then ask yourself, "Does this feeling, whatever it is, make me feel good or bad? Is this something I want more of, or not?" Try to reduce the feeling to a simple yes or no. Learn to recognize when something feels off.

"You know the truth by the way it feels."
—Unknown

Have you ever been in a situation where you felt upset, but you couldn't logically figure out why? You have no good reason to feel out of sorts but, nevertheless, you do. Don't try to justify your feelings. Don't try to rationalize whether or not you "should" be feeling that way. It doesn't have to make sense. You are where you are.

When you are unsure about a feeling, try to determine if it feels expanded or contracted. Does it feel heavy or light? Do you feel ahead of the curve, or behind it?

You know the feeling of driving your car down a curvy road on a warm summer day. You're confident and familiar with the road. You've got the music blaring, the windows are down, and you are steering back and forth around the curves and singing at the top of your lungs. You *feel* ahead of the curve—like you can't go fast enough. You *feel* open, expanded, and sure. Think about the way that feels and let that resonate within you.

Now think about how this situation feels. You're driving the same car on an unfamiliar, curvy road late at night in the pouring rain. You can't see two feet in front of you. The road is narrow, and you come up on a curve a little too fast. You feel out of control, tense, and you have a white-knuckled grip on the steering wheel. You *feel* like the car is ahead of you. It's practically dragging you. Your shoulders are tight. You feel hesitant, unsure, and contracted. Now let that feeling resonate.

As you move to the lower end of the emotional scale, it will feel like resistance, not ease. You will feel like you are struggling against the current—exhausting, uncomfortable, and panic-stricken. Not only are you out of the flow, but you are pushing against who you are on a soul level. It's a difficult, cloudy, confusing feeling. You know you are moving away from Source when you are feeling those uncomfortable feelings.

"If it lowers your vibration, it's not for you. That's how you'll know."

—Lalah Delia

When you are in the flow of Source, you will feel light-hearted and inspired. Open and expanded. You will feel at ease. It will feel like the next logical step. It's the difference between hammering a puzzle piece into place or having it click effortlessly together.

Like the old Morris Albert song, "It's feelings—nothing more than feelings." Feelings, and not words, are the indication of your vibrational frequency level. When you can pinpoint the feeling and emotion of it, you have nailed the vibration of it.

It's important to remember that wherever you are on the scale isn't good or bad. It's just information. It's just your GPS letting you know which direction you're headed in. Source doesn't get pissed that you're pushing against the current. Source is always flowing and always the same. You are the one who moved vibrationally, the one who changed direction. You're the one feeling the disconnection. And you and you alone have the power to turn around and get to a better-feeling place. You can go with the flow or continue to push against it. Widen the gap or close it. It's up to you.

"Your heart
knows the way.

Run in that
direction."
RUMI

shad·ow
/'SHadō/

noun

1. a dark area or shape produced by a body coming between rays of light   and a surface.
   "trees cast long shadows"

2. used in reference to proximity, ominous oppressiveness, or sadness and gloom.
   "the shadow of war fell across Europe"

"Only in
the darkness
can you see
the stars."

MARTIN LUTHER KING, JR.

Shadow

Step 3—Why Negative Emotion Is Necessary

So, let's talk about negative emotion. When you are attracting unwanted things into your life, does that mean you're doing something wrong? Is it even possible to live your life and avoid ever feeling disconnected from Source? Absolutely not. You are walking around in this human body to experience the wholeness and richness of life. You came here to get your hands dirty.

Negative emotion is part of the natural rhythm and process of life. It just is. There's no such thing as a life lived without some degree of upheaval and uncertainty. You would not even be able to feel happiness if you didn't have the capacity to experience sadness. One cannot exist without the other. According to the Laws of Relativity and Polarity, to do so is virtually impossible.

The Universal Law of Relativity states that nothing (thought, person, emotion, action, etc.) can be evaluated unless you can compare it in relation to something else. Light cannot exist unless there is darkness. One simply cannot be without the other. Think about a photograph. If you don't have the different values of light and dark, it's just blank—it's nothing.

Without some degree of contrast, there is nothing to see.

Similarly, the Law of Polarity states that everything exists in duality, meaning that everything has two extreme ends of the same spectrum. For example, let's use hot and cold. Although they are opposites, they are on the same continuum, and one cannot exist without the other. How can you know what hot feels like if you don't know how it feels to be cold? There are two sides to every subject. There is either the presence of it or the absence of it with varying degrees in between. There has to be some degree of contrast for anything to have any meaning at all.

When I was growing up, my family went to a typical Southern Baptist Church that taught the "get saved or go to Hell" type of theology. If you believed and played by the rules then when you died, you would get to go to heaven. Heaven being described as a crystal city with streets of gold up in the sky with angels floating around. As a child, I remember being as afraid of going to heaven as I was of going to hell. Even if it were my idea of paradise—and it definitely was not—why would I want to spend an eternity in a place with no variety or diversity? I felt like Mark Twain when he said, "If I cannot drink bourbon and smoke cigars in heaven, then I shall not go." Even at a young age, I instinctively knew that when there is no invariability of anything without something to compare it to, it then loses its value.

> *"If you strive only to avoid the darkness or cling to the light, you cannot be in balance. Try striving to be conscious of all that you are."*
>
> —Gary Zukav

It's the same thing with your feelings and emotions. The goal is not to eliminate negative emotion from your experience but to understand what those emotions are telling you. Remember, the way you feel is just an indication of where you lie on the emotional scale.

Negative emotion is important because it is letting you know what you do not want. It is on the same spectrum of what you "do" want, but that uncomfortable feeling is letting you know that you are moving away from it or are experiencing the lack of it. It's like a speed bump or a signpost guiding you in a different direction.

> *"If you aren't in over your head, how do you know how tall you are?"*
>
> —T.S. Eliot

Instead of thinking of negative emotion as bad, try to think of it as being like the nerve endings in your body that allow you to feel pain. We don't want to feel physical pain, but it's beneficial information if you happen to put your hand down on a hot stove. You need to know you're in danger in order to protect yourself. It's helpful to have that pain to let you know to pull your hand away as quickly as possible before it burns to a crisp. Negative emotion serves the same purpose. Isn't it nice to have some kind of warning device to let you know you're in trouble before you find yourself stranded on the side of the road?

Let's say you are having a personal experience that feels muddy, chaotic, and confusing. Then you will be hesitant to continue to move in that direction. If it feels clear, exciting, and interesting, then moving in that direction will feel natural.

It will feel like the next logical step. Maybe you don't have a significant feeling one way or the other. Don't worry; if it's not for you, the feelings will become more intolerable. As the negative emotion intensifies, you will know to adjust.

Sometimes we have to let things get really uncomfortable before we will pay attention and take a different direction. As long as we will put up with, or tolerate, what we do not want, we will usually do just that. It's like having a pebble in your shoe. You're walking through life and something doesn't feel quite right, but you will shift your weight to avoid doing anything about it. It has to get really painful before you will stop, take your shoe off, and shake the pebble out. If you refuse to pay attention to what your guidance system is alerting you to then a little pebble in your life can become a huge-ass boulder.

When you are in the middle of pain and adversity, it can be hard to focus on anything else. Especially when you have a damn good reason to feel the way you do. There are countless justifiable reasons to feel anger, hatred, grief, etc. I get it. You're not wrong. You did get a raw deal. They could have treated you better. It wasn't fair. It absolutely does suck.

> *"I'm trying to be a more positive person every day.*
> *Today, I'm positive everyone is an asshole."*
>
> —Unknown

I know you've heard the expression, "when it rains, it pours," meaning when things go south, they can really take a nosedive. You find yourself in an energetic, downward spiral. You've come up on a metaphorical speed bump, but instead of looking at it as a directional tool showing you that you should what (and I can't stress this enough) the fuck.

~~UNKNOWN~~

EVERYBODY AT SOME POINT

take another path, you just bitch about having to slow down. You lose your job and all you can talk about is how unfair it was and how nothing ever works out for you. You get rear-ended on the freeway. You find out your husband is leaving you for somebody else. And all these things just reaffirm that you have a bullseye on your back and the whole world is using you for target practice. The more you dwell on your predicament, the more evidence shows up to prove that you are right.

The irony is that the more you focus and dwell on what you don't want and hate about what's going on, the more you will attract those kinds of things into your experience. You can't expect a positive outcome as long as you are focused on the negative aspects of a situation.

It's one thing to talk about being in a state of negative emotion intellectually from a broader perspective; it's another thing to be up close, wallowing in the feeling of the heaviness of it. You know what I mean—the way it actually feels. That feeling of being punched in the gut, of the rug being pulled out from under you, of something coming into your life that is so unwanted you feel as though an elephant is standing on your chest. You can hardly breathe.

You can't ignore that feeling. It wouldn't do any good to deny it anyway. That's the way you feel. You are where you are, and where you are at that moment sucks. Own it. Feel the pain, feel the anger, feel the revenge. Sometimes you need to stew, regurgitate, and wallow in it. As my mother used to say, "Sometimes we're not happy unless we're miserable."

"I'll get over it. I just gotta be dramatic first."
—Unknown

"I never make the
same mistake twice.

I make it like five
or six times, you know,

just to be sure."

DAN HOOKER

Some people live their whole lives churning around in varying degrees of this tornado of negativity. But you don't have to. This pushing against, disconnected, closed-off way of navigating and living life feels so awful that, if you're lucky, "the how you got there" becomes inconsequential. You literally get sick and tired of being sick and tired. All you want is relief.

Getting to the point of surrender is a really good place to be. You aren't giving up in the sense that whatever wrong has been done to you is forgivable or even ok. It just means that nothing is worth losing your connection to Source. Source didn't desert you. It's been right there the whole time, communicating and leaving you breadcrumbs along the way. But you can't see the signs from a state of hate and revenge. That's not where Source lives and you can't connect to Source from those lower vibrations.

You may have every justifiable reason imaginable to feel hate and revenge towards someone, but at the end of the day, the only one it is hurting is you. Your ex-husband has a new girlfriend, and someone else is sitting at your old desk at your old job. Whether it was wrong or right doesn't matter; you have to let it go, to move beyond it. By holding on to the negativity, you and you alone are the only stumbling block in your path that does not allow you to realize the expansion that those experiences inspired within you.

> *"Your current situation is giving you an opportunity to re-evaluate what you want."*
>
> —Tashabee

The expansion to move beyond "what is." Think about that. If you will try to put things in perspective and stop

I've never seen any life transformation that didn't begin with the person finally getting tired of their own bullshit."

ELIZABETH GILBERT

"WHEN LIFE SHUTS A
DOOR...OPEN IT AGAIN.

IT'S A DOOR.

THAT'S HOW THEY WORK."

UNKNOWN

looking at what you've lost, you might see that although you thought your marriage was the be-all end-all, if it were meant to be, —it would be. Maybe your ex was a douchebag and had been cheating on you all along; maybe he is a really nice guy but you both want different things; maybe you will take the things you learned from that relationship and go on to have a more fulfilling one. And what about that job? Was that really the job of your dreams? Wouldn't you enjoy a job that pays more and gives you more freedom? Let that shit go. You can't get to where you want to go by remaining where you are.

Every negative experience and struggle can be viewed as an opportunity for growth and expansion. By consciously stepping back from a difficult situation and trying to see it as a lesson learned and not a defeat, you automatically take yourself out of the victim mindset. You become a co-creator, acting in harmony with Source within you. And from this connected state of being, now you can trust the guidance and the breadcrumbs. Letting go of the resistance to the problem allows you to open up to the perfect orchestration and synchronicity of the Universe working on your behalf. When you stop focusing on the problem, you will begin to see the solution.

> "~~Why is this happening to me?~~
> What is this teaching me?"
>
> —Unknown

That's why mistakes and failures aren't the opposite of success. They are necessary for success. They are part of the clarifying process. Until you live, observe, and have the experiences of wanted and unwanted, how do you know? There would be no growth and expansion without the contrasting experiences that cause you to have the desire to move beyond where you are. And expansion is what it's all about. There's no going back.

> *"Try not to resist the changes that come your way. Instead, let life live through you. And do not worry that your life is turning upside down. How do you know that the side you are used to is better than the one to come?"*
>
> —Rumi

Your consciousness is constantly expanding. You are observing life from a different vantage point incrementally as you grow and have different experiences. Therefore, your wants and desires are evolving as well. You aren't consciously choosing as if you were ordering a life out of a catalog, but you are automatically fine-tuning your preferences in reaction to what you are experiencing. The expansion to become more is necessary for growth and fulfillment. That's the joy of life.

In the rockumentary "The History of the Eagles," when being interviewed about the turmoil of being in one of the most famous rock-n-roll bands of its time, Joe Walsh was quoted as saying, "You know, there's a philosopher who said, as you live your life—it appears to be anarchy and chaos, and random non-related events, smashing into each other and causing this situation or that situation. And then this happens and it's overwhelming, and it just looks like—what in the world is going on? And then later, when you look back on it, it looks like a finely crafted novel . . . But at the time—It don't!"

We can't see the big picture when we are in the midst of it.

"...you can't connect the dots looking forward; you can only connect them looking backwards. So you have to trust that the dots will somehow connect in your future. You have to trust in something—your gut, destiny, life, karma, whatever.

This approach has never let me down, and it has made all the difference in my life."

STEVE JOBS

It's like standing two inches away from the side of an elephant and trying to make sense of what's in front of you. You're too close. All you can see is a wall of gray, wrinkly skin. Not the magnificent beast that is the whole of it. Shadow is like that. It's only part of the puzzle. Don't make it out to be more than it is.

Trust that there is a greater plan behind the scenes. Allow life to flow through you without feeling the need to judge every event as good or bad, or right or wrong. We all experience suffering and loss at some point in our lives. It is our need to question, analyze, and internalize the difficulties in life that actually causes us to suffer. Pain is inevitable but suffering is optional. It is your ability to control how you respond to adversity that determines how it will impact you. You get to decide if it's a lesson, a detour, a roadblock, or if the whole damn road is washed out. You get to choose what it means for you.

Our lives are perfectly imperfect. Think about it. Would you go see a movie if there was no plot or storyline? No obstacles to overcome, no feelings of accomplishment? Don't you enjoy playing or watching a sport more if there is tension and competition? Why do you think the line to ride the rollercoaster is always the longest? It's for the thrill of the ride! We thrive on it. It's the drama, the highs and the lows, the diversity, and the choices that give life color and meaning. Nothing is ever going wrong. It's part of the process of becoming more. You are right on track.

Breathe through the hard times and trust that it is just a phase of your story. Believe that the dots are connecting, and things are working out in your favor. No matter how dark and heavy shadow feels in the moment, it is only temporary. It does not have to define you. Trust that even the darkest night will end, and the sun will rise again.

"Life is amazing. And then it's awful.
And then it's amazing again. And in
between the amazing and the awful it's
ordinary and mundane and routine.
Breathe in the amazing, hold on
through the awful, and relax and exhale
during the ordinary. That's just living
heartbreaking, soul-healing, amazing,
awful, ordinary life.

And it's breathtakingly beautiful."

L.R. KNOST

re·lease
/rəˈlēs/

verb

1. allow or enable to escape from confinement; set free.

2. allow (something) to move, act, or flow freely. "she released his arm and pushed him aside"

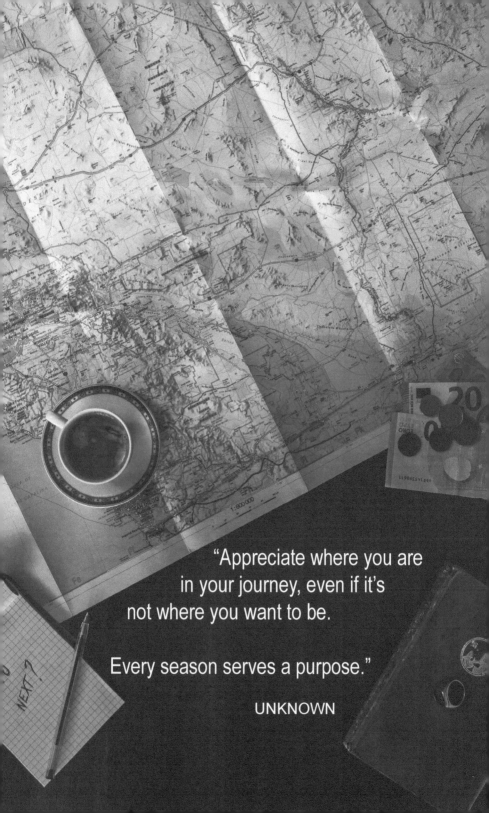

"Appreciate where you are
in your journey, even if it's
not where you want to be.

Every season serves a purpose."

UNKNOWN

Release

Step 4—Making Peace with What Is

So, let's say you're swirling around in a shitstorm of negative energy and emotion. But as long as you're focused on what went wrong and why you're in the middle of this shitstorm, the "Law of Attraction" is just going to match you up with more shit. And the more shit you experience, the more angry and bitter you become—thus the more shit you have to deal with. Did I mention that you're angry and bitter? I mean, a mad at the world, elephant on your chest, can't breathe, fury.

You have an internal dialogue going on in your head that simply will not turn off. If you aren't obsessing over what went wrong in the past, you're worried about what could go wrong in the future. If you're thinking about the present moment, you are judging what is, quick to point out what is wrong with everybody and everything. There isn't enough time, there isn't enough money, everybody is out to get you, the news is so depressing, and on and on and on.

So, what do you do with that? You're not enjoying it. In fact, you hate it. You don't want to feel that way, but that's the way you feel and that's all there is to it. What do you do when, basically, you are churning around in a negative spin cycle of shit?

First of all, you don't have to know one thing about energy, the emotional scale, or Universal Laws to know that all you want is to feel relief from those terrible feelings. Those lower vibrational emotions feel . . . well, like shit. Nobody wants to feel that way. And we will do whatever we can to turn off the incessant mind chatter and numb those unwanted feelings. You will do whatever it takes not to *feel* them. Abusing alcohol and drugs, destructive behavior towards yourself or other people, making someone else hurt more than you are hurting, are all knee-jerk responses to deal with those uncomfortable feelings.

> *"People are not addicted to alcohol or drugs, people are addicted to escaping reality."*
>
> —Unknown

Does that work? Hell yeah, it works. Momentarily, you will feel a sense of relief. But it's just a temporary reprieve that can't help but bring more shit to the storm, because you haven't moved to a better-feeling place, you've just found a way to tolerate being in the shitstorm. To get out of the shitstorm, you first have to move vibrationally. And to do that, you are going to have to find a way to feel better about being in a shitty situation—and that's not an easy thing to do.

How do you begin to neutralize those unwanted feelings? Being in denial or just changing the language you use won't work, because feelings don't lie. You feel angry and bitter. You can't instantaneously go from angry and bitter to calm and peaceful, but you can take baby steps to incrementally shift and begin to move in a more positive direction.

"Acceptance doesn't mean resignation; it means understanding that something is what it is and that there's got to be a way through it."

MICHAEL J. FOX

What we're looking for here is the feeling of release. It's actually the feeling of pushing against the current vibrationally that feels so uncomfortable. The unwillingness to accept where you are and railing against the circumstances that got you there only serve to hold you in that painful vibration. You can't move beyond it until you can find a way to let go of it. To begin to change how you feel about it, you have to adjust your perspective. You have to find a way to look at the situation and create a dialogue with yourself that makes it ok. I'm not saying that it's ok that it happened, but you have to find a way to feel ok, in spite of it.

> *"Staying positive does not mean that things will turn out okay. Rather, it is knowing that YOU will be okay no matter how things turn out."*
>
> —Unknown

You have to find a way to make peace with "what is." Because really, what other choice do you have? It is what it is. And you can't change "what is" by remaining where you are. You have to take away the only thing that is allowing it to remain in your experience and that is your attention to the unwanted aspects of it.

You have to take control of the negative self-talk that is on a constant loop in your head. Instead of your mindless, reactionary thoughts running the show, you are going to be selective about the thoughts you entertain. Create an internal dialogue with yourself that brings you peace instead of one that feeds your anxiety. It's not "what they're doing" that is messing with your peace—it's what you're "*thinking* about what they're doing." You can't control what they're doing but you can control

"Being negative only makes a difficult journey more difficult. You may be given a cactus, but you don't have to sit on it."

JOYCE MEYER

how you choose to think about it.

Before you can begin to rewire your thinking and stop the shitty spin cycle of negative thoughts that you have going on in your head, you have to stop their momentum.

Zen Buddhists refer to the constant chatter of thoughts in your head as the "monkey mind." It's as though your thoughts are swinging from branch to branch like a bunch of drunken, unsupervised monkeys. Right now, you're jumping from one anxiety-ridden thought to the next. It's exhausting. No matter where you go, you can't get away from these thoughts. There's no escaping them. How do you shut it off?

> *"I literally cut myself off in the middle of a negative thought like—Girl! We don't have time for this!"*
>
> —Unknown

Initially, instead of trying to put a positive spin on anything, just try to shut your thoughts off. Try to shut the negative chatter down, period. You are looking for a way to calm the monkey mind. This is where meditation can be really helpful. And when I say meditation, I don't just mean sitting in the lotus position in complete silence. Although if that works for you, by all means, do that.

There isn't one right way to do this. There's no one right way to do anything; why should this be any different? Just try to find something you can focus on that you have no judgment about and try to zone out. Focus on the ticking of a clock, concentrate on the hum of the air conditioner, stare at the flame of a candle, count your breaths in and out. Be mindful of quieting your mind. Be intentional. Listen to a guided meditation app on your phone. Sit quietly in your car. Put on your headphones and take a walk. Play the guitar. Paint. Go for a hike. Soak in a hot bath. The secret is to find out what works for you.

As you try to quiet your mind, thoughts will continue to come up. You're not doing it wrong if your mind isn't completely blank. When a thought comes up or your mind begins to wander, just gently take your attention back to the sound, the flame, the music, or whatever you're using and start again. Think of your mind like a puppy that you are trying to train to sit. Every time the puppy gets up, you take him back to the same spot and sit him down again, over and over and over. Just like the puppy will finally get the message to sit, your thoughts will start to slow down as well.

Once you have quieted your mind and you have some semblance of control over your thoughts, you can begin to shift your perspective. See if you can find some aspect of your situation that can start to neutralize those negative feelings. Just the tiniest effort to move in the opposite direction and look for more positive thoughts will begin to open the flow of energy and lighten your mood. At this point, you aren't looking for a "twirling around on a mountain, deliriously happy, Julie Andrews" kind of feeling. You are looking for release. Baby steps. Incremental steps in a more positive direction.

Having a positive perspective doesn't mean that you are going to bury your head in the sand and be in denial. You're putting on rose-colored glasses, not blinders. You are just not going to give your attention to the things that you do not want. Just because something is true does not mean that it deserves your attention. Think about that.

You can't get rid of everything in the world that bothers you. You can't control the world or the behavior of the people

"Stop trying to calm the storm.

Calm yourself.

The storm will pass."

BUDDHA

in it, but you can control the way you respond to and how you
decide to feel about the world and the people in it. You can
control your focus and your vibration. That's the only thing
you *can* control. Get to the point that your personal vibration
and your connection to Source is your highest priority. And the
crap that you are fixated on, that is keeping you from feeling
good, is not worth the way you are allowing it to make you feel.
Let it go.

> *"Sometimes you don't realize the weight of something
> you've been carrying until you feel the weight of its
> release."*
>
> —Unknown

So, let's talk about what we're not going to focus on. That
sounds crazy, I know. How can you put a positive spin on something you do not want? How can you look at what you don't
want and find a way to feel good about it? Here are some strate-
gies to help you alter your perspective and try to see things in
a more beneficial way:

Adjusting Your Focus

You start by trying to find the best thought about it that
you can. You are going to have to actively look for it. Adjust
your focus until you can find some aspect of it that you can be
in agreement with—some angle on it that allows you to feel
that release of resistance.

Let's use this shitty situation as an example to illustrate
what I mean by adjusting your focus:

Let's say you're a struggling actor living in New York. You

are barely making it financially, working a string of waitressing and catering jobs. The service industry sucks and people can be so rude and don't tip well. You go on audition after audition but rarely get a call back. You aren't blonde and blue-eyed. You have an exotic look that seems to typecast you and limits your opportunities. You're really talented and it's so unfair. You are so tired of people holding you back. This is something you've dreamed of doing your whole life and yet, it's never going to happen.

As long as your focus is on the limitations of your situation, you're right. It's never going to happen. But what if you looked at it this way?

You live in New York, an amazing city! Opportunities are everywhere. You work in the food and restaurant industry. You never know who is going to walk through the door, who might sit at your table, who might be at the next party you work. You don't like waiting on rude people? Well, pretend. You're a fucking actor. Try out different accents, get into character while you're working. Make them believe you're having the time of your life. What better way to hone your craft? Expect to be discovered. Cinderella stories happen in show business every day. Why not you? You do have a different look, and in a sea of cookie-cutter blondes, you stand out. You're memorable. You're talented. Just because you aren't seeing immediate results doesn't mean that things aren't happening. The Universe is lining up synchronicities and circumstances to give you exactly what you want, but if you are so focused on why it's not happening, you aren't going to see them. You are only going to *see* what you decide to look for.

If focusing on the details of *how* it's going to work out makes you feel uncertain and insecure then back up your focus and go for the panoramic view. Go general. Things are always working out for you. Everything happens for a reason. Minding your personal vibration is the most important thing you can do to get you what you want. And in the present moment, you can do that. Find a way to feel good about where you are, right now. The details will take care of themselves if you are in the vibrational vicinity of what you want.

> *"Sometimes you need to give yourself a pep talk. Like, hello. You're a badass woman. Don't be sad. You got this and I love you!"*
>
> —Unknown

If You Don't Want It—Don't Think About It

We tend to think by worrying and railing against the unwanted things in our lives, we are pushing them away from us, but that's not how it works. Pushing against something is still giving it your attention. Vibrationally, you are asking the Universe for more of it. You get what you choose to think about. You can only access the level of frequency from which you are vibrating. It's attraction.

Mother Teresa was once quoted as saying, "I was once asked why I don't participate in anti-war demonstrations. I said I will never do that. But as soon as you have a pro-peace rally, I'll be there!" She understood that by focusing on the problems of the world, you are only making them expand in your reality. Be *for* a cause instead of *against* something unwanted. For example, instead of waging a war on drugs, be for early education and

MOST PEOPLE ARE
THINKING ABOUT WHAT
THEY DON'T WANT, AND
THEY'RE WONDERING
WHY IT SHOWS UP
OVER AND OVER AGAIN."

UNKNOWN

mentoring programs. Feel how just the reframing of that immediately takes the weight out of the problem and feels lighter.

Complaining, blogging, or explaining about how awful or unfair something is does not eliminate it from your experience. Focusing on the problem only makes the problem bigger. Shouting "No" at something does not make it go away. It can't, because by giving it your attention, you are either holding it in your vibration or holding what you want out of reach.

I have a personal experience that is a really good example of this. My husband and I had been married for about nine years when we decided to try to have a baby. Up until that time, he worked in the airline business and traveled a good bit and I worked full-time, so it just had not been on our radar. But now I was in my thirties, and I could hear the clock ticking. So, I stopped taking birth control pills.

I got pregnant right away. I was stunned. Given my age and how long I had been on the pill, I thought it might take a little while to get pregnant. I was still working full-time and now felt unsure about how I was going to handle my job and a baby. So, when I first found out I was pregnant, I was feeling overwhelmed and not exactly thrilled. But after several weeks I started to get excited. Then, at eight weeks . . . I miscarried. I lost the baby.

So, this baby, that I was a little ambivalent about initially, became all-consuming for me. We tried again as soon as we were able, thinking, *No problem, right?* I had gotten pregnant so quickly the first time but now—nothing. Month after month of counting days and taking my temperature, taking pregnancy test after pregnancy test, and still no baby. This went on for two more years. I was obsessed. All I could think about was that time was running out for me and I couldn't get pregnant.

My window was closing. I wanted a baby but couldn't have a baby. No baby. No baby.

Finally, after talking with my doctor, we came to the conclusion that the only other option we had would be to start fertility treatments. My husband and I talked about it, but by this time, we had been married for eleven years and we decided that maybe it just wasn't meant to be. So finally . . . I had let it go.

Less than a month after we made this decision, I was scheduled to have a minor surgery. When I went to the hospital the day before to do paperwork and pre-surgery testing, the nurse came out and told me that we would have to reschedule because—I was pregnant!

Are you getting what was happening here? I wanted a baby more than anything in the world, but my focus was on the "absence" of a baby in my life. The Universe was just responding to my vibration. We knew I could get pregnant. We knew my husband could get me pregnant. But because I was so focused on it not happening, I could not manifest a baby.

This experience totally illustrates the Universal Law of Polarity. Every subject is either the presence of something or the absence of it. And I was clearly vibrating on the "absence of baby" end of the spectrum. When I was trying to get pregnant, I wasn't excited. I was worried. I was anxious. I was pissed that it wasn't happening. BEEP, BEEP, BEEP—My emotional guidance system was clearly letting me know I was off the path of my desire, but I didn't understand that then. Only when I was able to let go of my focus on the problem was I able to allow my desire to flow to me.

The Law of Polarity applies to every single subject—love and hate, health and sickness, rich and poor, etc. The key is to put your focus on the wanted end of the spectrum. Decide what you are wanting to manifest and focus on aspects of that. But you are going to have to feel your way through. You have to get out of your head and pay attention to how your desires are making you feel, to know if you are on the right track.

Think About Something Else

What if you are all caught up in a bad-feeling thought? You're worried about upcoming layoffs at work, or you just received a bad scan result at the doctors, or you're afraid your kid is running around with a bad crowd, etc. These things are an "up in your face" reality for you. You have the awareness to know that these thoughts aren't beneficial to you, but as hard as you try, you can't seem to get to a better-feeling place about them.

It doesn't do you any good to try to work out the details of a puzzle that you don't even have all the pieces to. Worry is giving your attention to what you are in fear of, and not only does that not solve the problem, it attracts more of the same. Don't allow yourself to fall down the rabbit hole of worst-case scenarios. It's a dead end and it sure as hell won't bring you any comfort. Redirect and distract yourself to a completely different subject that you *can* feel good about.

> *"Worrying does not take away tomorrow's troubles. It takes away today's peace."*
>
> —Randy Armstrong

If you can't find a perspective about your situation that brings you any comfort then shift your thoughts to something else entirely. Use the discipline of your mind to redirect your thoughts to a completely different topic. Scarlett O'Hara was onto something when she said, "I can't think about that right now, I'll go crazy. I'll think about that tomorrow." Try to find something else, anything at all, that you can find some happiness and satisfaction about and try to focus on that. Do your best to stay off the unwanted subject and leave it alone.

Everything Is Not About You

We all have a tendency to think that everything that happens is personal to us; for example, someone cuts you off in traffic, you didn't like the bank teller's tone, your son has an attitude, you didn't get invited to that party, etc. When you automatically interpret someone's words and actions as a personal attack, you are making an assumption that you not only know what they are thinking but what they are thinking about you as well. Isn't it possible that they're just having a bad day? Maybe they just received some bad news. Maybe they're shy and awkward. It could be a million different things—all having not one thing to do with you.

Or maybe you're right. Maybe they don't like you. Maybe they *do* have malicious intent towards you. So what? If they *are* being vengeful or mean-spirited, you know that, from a vibrational standpoint, that is a really shitty place to be. I hate that for them. They deserve your compassion and understanding, not your retaliation.

They may have preconceived ideas about who you are, which may or may not even be true. They don't like your clothes, the color of your skin, your accent, who you hang out with, etc. Who cares? Another person's judgments have everything to do with them and nothing to do with you. What's more, it's none of your business.

"You can be the ripest, juiciest peach in the world.

And there's still going to be somebody who hates peaches."

DITA VON TEESE

They don't have to like you and you don't have to like them. You don't need their approval and they don't need yours. Our determination to get everybody on the same page, whether it be religion, politics, or whatever, is at the root of what creates so much unnecessary pain and resistance. We're all not the same and we're not supposed to be.

> *"Listen, smile, agree, and then do whatever the fuck you were gonna do anyway."*
>
> —Robert Downey, Jr.

Taking things personally and being offended has become a social norm in our society. We're offended if people use the wrong terminology, if differences in race and sex are noted, if differences in race and sex are ignored. How can we be politically correct when our politics are so varied and diverse? Don't get me wrong; I'm not saying people *should* say and do offensive shit. I'm saying they *are* going to say and do offensive shit. It's going to happen. You can't make everybody behave in a way that makes you feel more comfortable.

People are going to do what they're going to do, and *you* get to choose how you're going to react to that. Whether you choose to take offense and identify as a victim is up to you. You get to put it in a perspective that works for you. You can choose to believe that we are all human and fallible, and in most cases, we are doing the best we can, and we can feel that energy move in the direction of love and forgiveness. Or, we can choose to feel victimized, outraged, and angry and feel the pain of being disconnected from Source energy. It's not about them; it's about you and how you want to feel.

Have empathy and compassion, and don't be so quick to point the finger. Especially when every single one of us who chooses to throw rocks does so from the confines of a glass house. None of us is without fault.

We exist in an ever-evolving capacity. We are all just navigating through life in all of the knowledge and enlightenment that we have acquired up to this point in time. Don't judge them for their limited perspective, just like you hope and pray that you aren't being judged from where you currently stand. We all have a lot to learn.

Maybe you have views and beliefs about race, religion, politics, etc. that create an "us and them" mentality. Just because your mama told you that's the way it is, doesn't mean that point of view is working for you. How do those views make you feel? Where do those views place you on the emotional scale? How can something be right if it causes you to have feelings of hate or hostility? Recognize when your perceptions and beliefs aren't keeping you aligned with your higher self, and adjust accordingly.

Don't try to analyze your way through it; you have to feel your way. Don't get all caught up in crap like: well, they were on that land first, or they have all the oil, or if they would just work and not expect a handout, or they should have more respect, and so on.

We want so much to categorize everything into right and wrong, absolute piles. We want to judge others based on the perspective that we are coming from, and we get upset when they don't react to a situation like we would have. But as we talked about in the first section of this book, no two people have the same perspective.

You aren't going to find a person on earth that agrees with

"NORMAL IS AN ILLUSION. WHAT IS NORMAL FOR THE SPIDER IS CHAOS FOR THE FLY."

MORTICIA ADAMS

you about every single thing. Not the person you sleep with, not your best friend, not your parents, not your child, not your brother—nobody. You don't even agree with what you, yourself, thought five years ago. Maybe even five minutes ago. Stop trying to convince, debate, intimidate, and manipulate others into seeing your side. Let them do them and you do you.

The very definition of perspective states that there are many ways to see something based on the angle you choose to view it from. You have to find an angle that lines up with the connected-to-Source part of you. If a belief lowers your vibration then it's not serving you. Your alignment is your barometer.

Instead of focusing on our differences, shift your perspective to the similarities we share. One of my favorite illustrations of this principle is a video produced by TV 2 Denmark called "All That We Share." You can probably still find it on YouTube.

In the video, about a hundred people enter a large room that has been marked off into sections on the floor with tape. The people were divided into categories and then were told to stand with their group in each of the areas. There was the affluent-looking group, the low-income group, the tattooed streetwise group, the rural farmers group, the city dwellers group, the athletic group, the religious group, etc.—the Us and Them.

Then the facilitator told these groups of people that they were going to be asked some questions—some very personal ones—and if their answer was yes, they were to leave their assigned areas and go stand at the front of the room. The questions were things like: Were you the class clown in school? Are you a stepparent? Do you believe in life after death? Do you believe in UFOs? Do you like to dance? Did you have sex this week? Have you ever been bullied? Have you ever bullied someone else? Have you ever had your heart broken? Are you lonely? Etc.

All of these people, who in the beginning thought they were so different, began to see the similarities and the frailty of humankind in each other. They started to laugh, cry, encourage, and cheer each other on! You can literally see their faces soften and feel the energy open up between them. It is the absolute best video, and I cry every time I watch it. That "feel good" feeling is what we should be looking for in each other. It's there if we choose to see it.

There are so many similarities that we share. Why do we insist on harping on the differences that make us uncomfortable? We should look for commonality and respect that everyone is on their own journey and mind our own business, mind our own vibration.

You are the architect of your thoughts. Turn them around when you get off course. Consciously make the shift from unwanted to wanted, from outward to inward. Choose thoughts that bring you relief. Baby step by baby step, incrementally, shift to a better-feeling place.

"See the light in others,
and treat them as if
that's all you see."

—WAYNE DYER

vi·sion
/ˈviZHən/

noun

1. the faculty or state of being able to see.
   "she had defective vision"

2. the ability to think about or plan the future with imagination or wisdom.
   "the organization had lost its vision and direction"

"People generally see what they look for and hear what they listen for."

HARPER LEE

Vision

Step 5—Becoming a Deliberate Thinker

I'm a visual learner. I love lists, diagrams, illustrations, Pinterest pages, etc. I get a lot of satisfaction out of holding them in my hands, looking at them, and carrying them around with me. Notebooks full of drawings and ideas help me to "see" and understand. That's actually how this book started. It was more or less me just feeling so good about how this philosophy was coming together for me, that I just wanted to see it written out for my own personal satisfaction. I wanted to explain it, play with it, and reduce it down like a fraction to its lowest common denominator. That's when the rose-colored glasses metaphor began to strike a chord for me. I started to realize that whether we are looking at the panoramic picture or the microscopic details of any particular subject, we all have the ability to choose what we want to focus on. What we "choose" to see is the lowest common denominator. That's the key. No matter what your state of mind or your situation, you are always choosing.

It's like you're driving along the coast and on one side of you is the ocean. Waves are washing up on the sand, the sunlight is sparkling on the water like diamonds. Seagulls are soaring overhead and sandpipers are hopping along the shore. Pods of dolphins are playfully dancing in and out of the water. And then, on the other side of the road is a junkyard. A real eyesore, with old cars up on blocks and rusted out, dirty mattresses piled up, tin cans and trash scattered about.

Now you have two choices: you can obsess over the ugliness and unseemly sight of the junkyard or you can bask in the beauty and tranquility of the beach. You get to choose.

"The one that makes you the happiest. Pick that one."

—Unknown

You can say, "I can't enjoy the beach with all of that crap across the street. Somebody needs to clean that up first. I want to know who is responsible for that mess! I'm starting a petition. It's disgraceful. Not until it's cleaned up and justice has been served, will I be able to relax and enjoy the beach!"

And I say, ok . . . but the beach is right there. Look at the ocean. Look this way! Why focus on that when you can look over here? See the dolphins? Aren't they beautiful? This way— look over here! Why are you looking at that when you could just as easily look at the damn beach?

You can choose to focus on what's wrong across the street— why the world is in turmoil, how you don't approve of your neighbor's politics and life choices, if they would only, if they hadn't, she should have, he didn't, I don't have, and on and on and on. But why would you insist on looking at something that makes you miserable, when you could just as easily focus on something that makes you happier?

"I don't think of all the misery, but of the beauty that still remains."

—Anne Frank

You aren't in denial about the junkyard. It's real. There are some fucked-up things going on in the world and they're painful to look at. It's true. But at the same time, the world is also this beautiful, self-correcting miracle with so much more going right than wrong. That's real and true too. Decide you are going to give your attention to things that lift you up. If you feel inspired to clean up the junkyard then do that. But there is a difference in the feeling of being inspired and the feeling of pushing against what you do not want. Pay attention to the subtle distinction of that and move in the direction of the better-feeling thought. When you begin to look for the beauty and good in the world you can't help but find more evidence of it.

"Vision" is the art of reframing your view to one that holds you in alignment. It is, where to look and how to adjust your perspective in order to find a view that raises your vibration. Remember, everything you want is at the higher end of the vibrational scale and the only way to get there is to raise your personal vibration to meet it. Do whatever it takes to get there.

Look for the Extraordinary in the Ordinary

"Do not ask your children to strive for extraordinary lives. Such striving may seem admirable, but it is the way of foolishness. Help them instead to find the

wonder and the marvel of an ordinary life. Show
them the joy of tasting tomatoes, apples, and pears.
Show them how to cry when pets and people die.
Show them the infinite pleasure in the touch of a
hand. And make the ordinary come alive for them.
The extraordinary will take care of itself."

—William Martin

It's easy to get excited about the big things—the extraordinary moments, the big promotion, the new car, the birth of a child, etc. are all causes to celebrate. But don't get so caught up in waiting for the big moments to be happy that you miss the opportunities to be happy along the way. It's the journey, remember? We've all heard the expression, "Happiness is a journey, not a destination." But most of us are so pissed that we aren't where we want to be, that we fail to notice the precious, magical moments that are right in front of us.

Allow yourself to be easily impressed by the world and look at life as if everything is a miracle, because it is. Contemplate the phenomenon of the earth and the circle of life—our ecosystem, the various vegetation and terrain, billions of different species of life, all evolving, migrating, photosynthesizing, all adapting and mutating with an internal intelligence that coincides with the rhythm of the seasons and tides, the preciseness of the earth spinning in our atmosphere in perfect proximity to the sun for life here to flourish, the intricate detail of a spider's web or a bird's nest. Just the sheer beauty of nature. I mean, seriously? It's astounding!

Allow yourself to be in awe and inspired. Feel appreciation for music, art, great writers, and poets. Appreciate the amazing

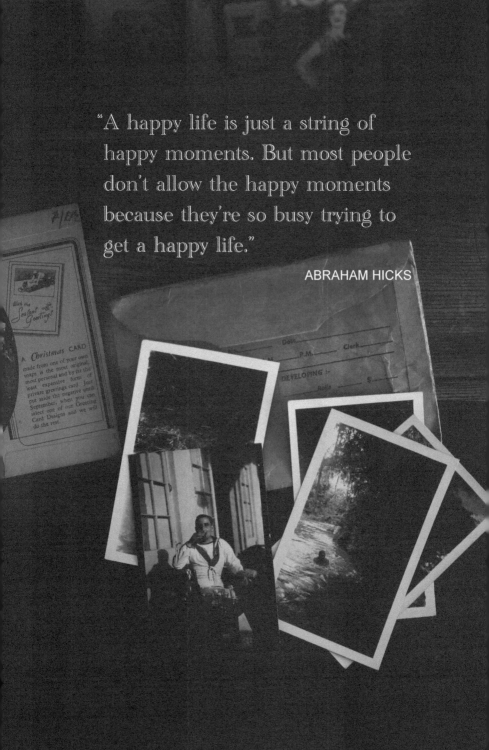

"A happy life is just a string of happy moments. But most people don't allow the happy moments because they're so busy trying to get a happy life."

ABRAHAM HICKS

talent of mere mortals to be able to capture the universal feeling of love or heartbreak and translate it into a few lines in a song or a passage in a book. Allow yourself to get lost in a piano chord or a guitar lick, pick apart the lyrics of a song, or be moved by a piece of art that touches your soul.

Marvel at the unbelievable lengths to which the human body can continue to defy logic and gravity. The excitement of seeing someone accomplish what was once thought impossible, and then see that record broken again and again. The manifestation of what man can imagine and create as our needs and resources evolve and change is truly amazing.

> *"Passion is energy. Feel the power that comes from focusing on what excites you."*
> —Oprah Winfrey

Pay attention to what thrills or excites you. Follow your passions. What is it that you want to read about or study for no other reason than that it interests you? What are you curious about? What makes you feel excited? It doesn't have to make sense. Follow the feeling. Whatever lights up the excitement, the love, the joy in you, will amp you up the emotional scale. Feel your way there by following one good-feeling impulse to the next one, and then the next. Purposely look for things that feed your soul and stoke them like a fire!

> *"Always go with your passions. Never ask yourself if it's realistic or not."*
> —Deepak Chopra

Let It Be More

I love a quote from the 1981 movie *Arthur*, where Dudley Moore is sitting at a bar, clearly drunk, and orders another round of drinks for him and his friend. The bartender asks him, "Haven't you had enough?" To which, Arthur replies, "I want more than enough!"

Don't we all? You are never going to get to a point in life where you are satisfied with what is, and not have any new desires. There is nothing wrong with wanting more, wanting better, wanting the improvement of whatever you currently have going on. That's just expansion. That's just life.

But to realize the expansion of what you want, you have to get in alignment with that expansion. You can't align with the improvement by complaining about where you are and bitching about what you don't have.

Remember to focus on the end of the spectrum that you are wanting to attract. You cannot attract abundance from a mindset of scarcity. A scarcity mindset is one of "not enough"—not enough time, not enough money, not enough resources, etc. It's the belief that life is like a big pie and there's only so much of it to go around. This creates a feeling of competition, a feeling of lack, and limited opportunities. In order for someone to win, someone has to lose. Think about how that feels. It makes your muscles tense. You feel anxious, powerless, and desperate. Not good.

Now think these thoughts: "The Universe is more than equipped to give me everything I want and need. There's more than enough to go around. Everything works out in perfect timing. I'm exactly where I need to be. I have so much to be grateful for. So much to appreciate." Now, how do those thoughts feel? You can literally feel your shoulders relax and

"Be thankful for what you have; you'll end up having more. If you concentrate on what you don't have, you will never have enough."

OPRAH WINFREY

your breathing slow down. Those thoughts feel good.

Practicing thoughts of gratitude and appreciation will raise your vibration by causing you to focus on the fullness of life rather than the lack. By aligning your thoughts to the things in your life that you are grateful for, you put yourself in a position to attract more of what you want.

Decide to look for things to be thankful for, no matter how small—the feeling of the sun on your face, clean sheets, a smile from a stranger, ice in your glass on a hot day, the smell of the rain as it hits the dry earth, etc. Make it a game. Make a list. Keep a journal. Be mindful of what you like and what is going right.

> *"The only healthy way to live life is to learn to like all the little everyday things—like a sip of good whiskey in the evening, a soft bed, a glass of buttermilk. Or a feisty gentleman like myself."*
>
> —Augustus McCrae

I once heard a woman on television talking about her morning ritual to start each day with gratitude. She said that when she wakes up, before her feet hit the floor, she is thankful to have been given another day. She gets in the shower and thinks about how fortunate she is to have running water and a water heater. The water that she is privileged enough to bathe in is cleaner than the drinking water for at least a quarter of the world's population. Not only is it clean but she just has to turn a handle and it comes right into her house. She didn't have to carry it from a creek or cut wood in order to heat it. She starts with that thought, letting the hot water warm her body, as she counts her blessings and sets her intentions for the day. I don't remember who she was or what I saw her on, but I never step foot in the shower without thinking about that. What a beautiful way to start the day!

No matter what you have going on in your life, I'm willing to bet you that you can think of at least one thing to be thankful for. Even if you have to look really hard for it. Be grateful for that. Dwell on that. Because focusing on that one thing is enough to shift your energy from lack to abundance. It's enough to begin to move in the direction of what you want.

> *"If your cup is only half full, you probably need a different bra."*
>
> —Unknown

Being grateful for what you have and appreciating things that you love, opens your heart and relieves the feeling of tightness in your body. It's the feeling of opening, the feeling of lightening up, the deep breath that you are looking for. Let it in. Open the valve and get in the flow to let it be more.

Embrace the Gray

To embrace the gray is to give up black-and-white thinking. Black-and-white thinking is a tendency to think in extremes. All or nothing. Right or wrong. Absolutes. This way of thinking suggests that there is a way to do things or a way to be, that is superior, and that way is the only way. There is no margin for error. It feels constricted and unforgiving. When the truth is, there is no such thing. There are exceptions to every rule.

"to be honest,
i'm just
winging it.
life,
motherhood,
my eye liner,
everything."

UNKNOWN

It's like life is a big classroom and we're all taking a test. But you can't cheat off your neighbor's paper, because everybody has a different test. Your journey is not their journey. Keep your eyes on your own paper. It's ok that you are struggling. It's ok that they are. How else are you going to learn?

We aren't supposed to have the answers for all the world's problems. Nobody is asking you to figure out everything for the world. You are just trying to figure out everything for you. And believe me, you've got your hands full with that. Give yourself and everybody else permission to be a work in progress.

Let go of the judgment of what you think it "should" be and accept that everybody and everything is in a state of becoming more. Be ok with the uncertainty and the imperfection of it all. Being open to, and ok with, not having all the answers is how the answers will come. When you are all caught up in the vibration of any problem, you are preventing the energy of the solution to come through. They are two very different vibrations.

Embracing the gray is like taking a "trust fall" with the Universe. It is leaning back and understanding that we live in a complex and uncertain world. It is trusting that there is a bigger picture and relaxing in the knowledge that things are always working out. Close your eyes, fall back, and trust that the answers will come when you are ready for them. That's what faith is.

"I wanted a perfect ending.
Now, I've learned, the hard way,
that some poems don't rhyme, and some
stories don't have a clear beginning,
middle and end.

Life is about not knowing,
having to change, taking the moment
and making the best of it, without
knowing what's going to happen next.
Delicious ambiguity."

GILDA RADNER

Life is Funny

> *"You find it offensive. I find it funny. That's why I'm happier than you are."*
>
> —Unknown

I say this from the bottom of my heart, with no disrespect intended whatsoever, but it would really be in all of our best interests to just . . . lighten the fuck up.

Honestly, few things in life will take you as far as a good sense of humor. There is nothing better than a heartfelt belly laugh with tears streaming down your face. Nothing. Laughter has been proven to reduce stress, boost your immune system, and lower your blood pressure. It is incredibly good for you, and it immediately lightens your mood.

Do whatever you can to see the hilarity in everyday life. Listen to a funny podcast, go to a comedy club, watch funny TV shows and movies, or amusing clips on YouTube or TikTok. I love one particular YouTube montage of news anchors messing up their lines or getting tickled on air. In half of the clips, you don't even know what they're laughing about, but their laughter is so contagious that you can't help but laugh too!

Surround yourself with funny, upbeat people who inspire and motivate you. Gravitate towards people who lift you up. Decide *you* are going to be one of those funny, upbeat people. Be the first one to smile, the first one to give a compliment. Be thoughtful. Be silly. Be kind, even if they aren't. Especially if they aren't—they need it more than anybody.

Don't take things so seriously, especially yourself. Acknowledge your flaws, shortcomings and mistakes with humor. We all do ridiculous, embarrassing things and have lapses

KINDNESS.

IT DOESN'T
COST A
DAMN
THING.

SPRINKLE
THAT SHIT
EVERYWHERE.

UNKNOWN

in judgement. Own it. Laughing at yourself when you screw up actually gives other people permission to feel like it's ok to be human and screw up too. There is a huge amount of freedom that comes to you when you don't care what others think about you.

Nora Ephron once said, "When you slip on a banana peel, people laugh at you. But when you tell people you slipped on a banana peel, it's your laugh." Let go of the feeling of having to defend and justify yourself. Let go of false pride. You can defuse a difficult or embarrassing situation for you, or them, simply by choosing to see the humor in it.

> *"Nothing is worth more than laughter. It is strength to laugh and abandon oneself. To be light. Tragedy is the most ridiculous thing."*
>
> —Frida Kahlo

Life can be absurd, a comedy of errors, so preposterous that you could not make it up. I can remember a time when it was just one terrible thing happening after another, and I thought to myself, *If I were watching this happen to a character in a movie, I would get up and walk out of the theatre. No one would believe it.* We've all had things happen like that. When things have gone so ridiculously off the rails that you literally had to laugh to keep from crying. It's one of those things you'll probably look back on and laugh about one day anyway; you may as well find a reason to laugh about it now.

Look Where You're Going, Not Where You've Been

Yes, whatever it is that happened, happened. It was hurtful. It was unfair. They had no right. You made a bad decision.

"I NEVER LOOK
BACK, DARLING.

IT DISTRACTS
FROM THE NOW."

EDNA MODE

They shouldn't have. You should have. But whatever happened, it's done. And you know what? It's over. Or is it?

As long as you go back and relive that hurt or regret, you are making a choice to keep it active in your vibration. It's still as painful as the day it happened, because you are choosing to keep it alive by giving it your attention. It's like a cut that can't heal because you keep going back and knocking the scab off. Stop touching it. Stop reliving it.

There's an old Buddhist parable that illustrates this perfectly. There were two traveling monks who came upon a river where they met a young and very attractive woman. She was in despair. She had to cross the river but was afraid to do so. The current was too strong and she was afraid of drowning. Without hesitation, the older monk picked her up, put her on his shoulders, and carried her across the river. Arriving safely on the other bank, he sat her down and bowed. She expressed her gratitude and departed. The monks continued their journey in silence. Unable to hold his silence any longer, the younger monk spoke with reproach, "Master, you, of all people, should have known that our spiritual teaching forbids us contact with women, and yet, you picked that one up and carried her on your shoulders! How can that be?"

"Brother," replied the master, "I put her down on the other side of the river hours ago; you're the one who's still carrying her."

You may struggle with forgiving others for the wrongs done to you or even struggle with forgiving yourself for regrets but holding onto them keeps you from moving beyond them. You can't create a new story if you keep retelling the old one.

"Guilt, regret, resentment, grievances, sadness,

*bitterness, and all forms of non-forgiveness are caused
by too much past and not enough presence."*

—Eckhart Tolle

If it's not happening right now, in the present moment, then it's water under the bridge and no amount of guilt or regret is going to change one damn thing about it. You can't un-ring the bell. It's done. It's over. But the present moment is an opportunity to change your perspective. It's new and untainted, a fresh start. Get in the driver's seat and decide where you want to go from where you are now.

*"I did what I knew how to do. Now that I know
better, I do better."*

—Maya Angelou

If you are looking in the rearview mirror of life, try to see painful experiences as lessons learned and appreciate how everything you've been through has gotten you to where you are today. Forgive them, not because they deserve it, but because you do. Forgive yourself because you love yourself enough to care about the way you feel. Try to stay focused in the present moment. Resolve not to travel down memory lane unless you can look back with love, with nostalgia, with peace. If you have memories that warm your heart and bring a smile to your face, then milk them for all they are worth. If it's uplifting to look back, then hell yes, do that. But if you look back and it feels heavy—make a conscious decision to leave that baggage in the past where it belongs. Love yourself enough to let that shit go.

The Preview of Coming Attractions

> *"Without leaps of imagination, we lose the*
> *excitement of possibilities. Dreaming, after all is a*
> *form of planning."*
>
> —Gloria Steinem

The dictionary describes imagination as the ability to imagine things that are not real, the ability to form a picture in your mind of something that you have not seen or experienced, and the ability to think of new things. Imagination is the ability to visualize beyond what is. It's a tool used to create something out of nothing. It's the first step in the process of thoughts becoming things. Think about it. Every single thing that has been created by man started with a spark of imagination, an idea.

Thoughts are powerful. Since your thoughts are made of energy and like energies attract, this means that even what you choose to think about the future has a bearing on what will actually manifest for you. You get what you think about. Whether it's the past, present, or future.

It's kind of like a superpower, right? If you consistently imagine and visualize a future event then you have a hand in sparking the creation of that. It is a preview of things to come. You are "pre-paving" a path for that scenario to manifest. So . . . what are you going to do with that? Are you going to use this superpower for good or for evil?

> *"Worry is a misuse of imagination."*
>
> —Dan Zadra

Worry is essentially visualizing and attracting the very thing that you do *not* want. It is imagining the worst-case scenario. It's fear of what *might* happen. You know what I'm talking about. You worry about your kid getting in a car accident, you're worried that you're going to get COVID-19, you're worried you won't have enough money for retirement, etc. Keep in mind now, these things haven't happened. Not yet. But nevertheless, you feel anxious and uneasy. You can't sleep. Your monkey mind is bouncing these anxious thoughts around like a pinball machine. Not where you want to be.

Now, I'm not making light of anxiety and depression. It's real, man. I myself have experienced panic attacks that would come on, out of the blue, for no apparent reason. When I was pregnant with my son, I would spontaneously break out in hives and go into anaphylactic shock. The doctor couldn't find a medical explanation for it. I get what it feels like for unwanted emotions to be driving your car. Obviously, I had some subconscious shit going on.

The thing is, it doesn't matter how you got out there on the ledge; it's what you're going to do about it in the present moment. It is what it is. You're apprehensive and fearful. Whether it's a rational thought or not, you feel like you're having a fucking heart attack. All you want is relief.

> *"We suffer more in imagination than in reality."*
> —Seneca

Talking about how you got out there on the ledge is just going to hold you there. So, don't do that. You don't want to *feed* the anxiety; you want to stop the momentum so you can turn this thing around. So, you're going to have to talk yourself off the ledge like you would a suicide jumper.

You're at first, going to pull out your "release" bag of tricks. Do your best to quiet your mind. If you can't sleep, get up and take a walk or watch a movie. Have a glass of wine or do a crossword puzzle. Distract yourself. If you need help in dealing with the physical response to anxiety then take medication, but medication will just relieve the physical symptoms, you still have to find a way to move vibrationally.

Soothe yourself. Talk to yourself like you would a friend—Has your kid been in a car accident? Not today. Do you have COVID-19? I hope not, but if you do, you have a miraculous body with an immune system that is built to fight disease and bacteria. Visualize that—not succumbing to the virus. Are you retiring today? Most likely not. Hell, you may not live to be old enough to retire. Are you going to ruin what time you have by worrying about something that you may not even need? Ok, maybe that last thought was a bad example. My point is, whatever you are struggling with, ask yourself, "Is it relevant today? Has it happened today?" Stay in the present moment. Today is all that you have to manage.

Better yet, use your superpower for good. It works both ways. Instead of imagining the worst-case scenario, fantasize about all the things that could go right. You could just as easily imagine your kid pulling safely into the driveway every night. Imagine you and your family vibrant and healthy. Imagine doors opening and resources being available when you need them. If you're going to let your imagination run wild, let it work for you, not against you. Imagine the most beautiful life you can conjure up.

"Let's conjure up from the depths of our souls: the truest, most beautiful lives we can imagine. The truest, most beautiful families we can fathom. The truest, most beautiful world we can hope for. Let's put it all on paper. Let's look at what we've written and decide that these are not pipe dreams; they are our marching orders. These are the blueprints for our lives, our families, and the world. May the invisible order become visible. May our dreams become our plans."

—Glennon Doyle

Instead of dread, choose to feel hopeful. Choose to feel anticipation and expectation. Make a vision board. Make lists. Make plans. Get specific about your dreams as long as it feels good to fill in the details. If filling in the details makes you feel anxious because you can't figure out how it's ever going to happen, then back up and look at it generally, from a panoramic view. Everything is working out perfectly for you. You don't have to know everything today. The pieces are falling into place. Feel your way to peace.

Imagery and visualization have long been used as motivational tools. Athletes describe seeing the ball going through the hoop or dropping into the hole in their mind's eye, before ever physically attempting the shot. Performers imagine the sound of applause before they reach the stage. Salespeople imagine customers needing their products and meeting goals before they make the first sale. If you can imagine it, you can manifest it. Anything can happen. Anything happens all the time. Imagine the best possible scenario for your life, and then expect to get it.

"I WANT IT ALL–
AND I WOULD
LIKE IT
DELIVERED."

BETTE MIDLER

Here's Your Sign

The "Law of Inspired Action" states that everything is connected. And because we are all part of the "all that is," we all have the ability to tap into that collective consciousness. We all have the ability to receive inspiration for action, intuitively.

Call bullshit on that if you want to, but you all know that you've experienced it. We've all had that feeling of just knowing. You've had a feeling in your gut, an inner voice nudging you in the direction of where you needed to be. You went back in the house for no logical reason and discovered you had left the stove on. You thought of someone you haven't talked to in years and then, miraculously, they cross your path. You experience déjà vu. You've dreamed this. You get a familiar, warm feeling. You get a weird, something-is-off feeling. You meet someone new and yet it feels like you have known each other for years. There's an instant connection—like, there you are; I've been looking for you.

These things are not random. Everything is connected. Everything is made up of energy coming from that same energetic Source. There is an internal knowing, an intuitive guidance system, that you can tap into that will steer you in the right direction, if you are open to following the signs and the breadcrumbs along the way.

> *"Your intuition knows her shit."*
>
> —Unknown

Just like you have to get really sensitive to the way you are feeling and pay attention to the nuances of your emotions, you also have to sharpen your senses to notice the signs and signals you are receiving. Remember, Source is always the same. The breadcrumbs are already there. You are always being guided. It may not be a burning bush or a crack of thunder with an audible voice saying, "Go to the store and buy a lottery ticket at 12:02 p.m." Well, I guess it could be, and if that happens, I would certainly heed that advice. But if you are waiting for the "Hollywood CGI, big-budget production" sign then you are going to miss what the Universe is laying down. It's random, but deliberate. It's subtle, yet obvious.

It's kind of like the joke about the guy on the roof. This fellow was stranded on the rooftop of his house during a flood. He was praying to God for help. Soon, a man in a rowboat came by and shouted to the man on the roof, "Jump in; I can save you." The stranded man shouted back, "No, it's ok; I'm praying to God and he's going to save me." So, the rowboat went on. Then a motorboat came by. The fellow in the motorboat shouted, "Jump in; I can save you." But the man on the roof said, "No, thanks; I'm praying to God and he's going to save me. I have faith." So, the motorboat went on. Then a helicopter came by and the pilot shouted down, "Grab this rope and I will lift you to safety." To this, the stranded man again replied, "No, thanks; God will save me. I have faith." So, the helicopter reluctantly flew away. Soon the water rose above the rooftop and the man drowned. He went to Heaven. When he met God, he said, "I had faith in You but You didn't save me; You let me drown. I don't understand why." To this, God replied, "What are you talking about? I sent you two boats and a helicopter!"

Picking up signs and signals is all about being in conversation with everything around you—seeing repeating numbers or patterns. Synchronicities, like hearing a song on the radio

"If you ask the Universe to send you signs,

believe what shows up."

UNKNOWN

that has the exact lyrics you need to hear at the perfect moment or someone crossing your path right when you need them. Finding or losing objects. Repeatedly seeing an object like a coin or a feather. Electrical or technical malfunctions, like the lights flickering on and off. Roadblocks, detours, or delays that end up keeping you from danger or putting you exactly where you need to be. Lucid dreams. Gut feelings—you don't know how you know, but you just know. Things falling perfectly into place or everything going wrong. All of these things may seem insignificant and coincidental but think about what is going on with you when these types of things occur. It's like a wink from the Universe, saying, "I got you!"

> *"Your intuition is like a muscle, and the more you flex it, the greater it grows."*
>
> —Corin Grillo

When you experience these little winks, don't talk yourself out of it. Point blank, ask the Universe for help. Ask for a sign or a message. Be specific. Expect to get an answer. Play with it.

My mother passed away in 2013. She had struggled with poor health for years and had come to the point where in order to survive, she would need to have a major surgery. But the odds of her surviving the surgery were slim. So, either way, the prognosis was not good. They put her in the hospital for a week before the surgery to build up her strength and get her in the best shape that they could, to increase her chances to pull through. I was lucky to be able to spend a lot of time with her that week. We had the opportunity to talk about everything! She was ready for either outcome. She told me, it wasn't that she wanted to die, but if she couldn't have an improved quality of life then she was ready to go.

One night we were talking, and I said, "Let's make a deal. Whichever one of us dies first, let's decide to send each other a sign from the other side." I told her that just because she was having this surgery didn't necessarily mean that she would be the first to go. I could just as easily die in a car accident on the way home from the hospital that night. So, I told her if I were to die first, my sign to her would be a bird. A robin bird, because my name is Robyn. She thought for a second and said, "Well, then, I guess my sign will have to be a dog."

I told her, "Well, that's crazy, I see dogs all the time. How am I going to know which dog is a message from you?"

And she said, "You'll know."

A few days after we had this conversation, she had the surgery and as predicted, she never regained consciousness and died the following day. It was hard to lose her, but I actually had a great sense of closure and peace about it. It made me smile to think of her free from all of her health problems. I believe that we are all eternal, and even though her physical body was no more, I knew she still existed in some capacity, though my mind could not comprehend precisely how. She had always been very intuitive, especially with dreams, and I knew she would send me a message if she could.

A few weeks after the funeral, I get an insignificant e-mail from a customer rep about an order I had placed and the rep's name happened to be "Mitzi." And I thought, *Hmmm . . . Not a common name.*

Mitzi was the name of a dog that my grandfather had given my mother when she was pregnant with me. Mitzi was her baby before she had babies. Also, her father died from a heart attack when I was two weeks old, and my mother was only nineteen at the time. She always felt that as long as she had Mitzi, she still had a little part of her daddy alive with her. Mitzi lived to be fourteen years old and when she died, my father built a wooden box and encased her body in concrete because my mother wanted to make sure she could take Mitzi with her if we ever moved to another house. So as far as my mother was concerned, Mitzi was a pretty significant dog.

Still, there are numerous people in the world named Mitzi, right? Could just be a coincidence. A few days after that, I ran into a friend at Target, who was there shopping with a friend of hers from out of town. When she introduced her to me. . . you guessed it—her name was Mitzi! So, I'm like, ok this *is* the sign. It's definitely Mitzi!

A week or so later, I was taking shower in my bathroom in a house that, at that time, I had lived in for eight years. The shower in the master bathroom was tiled in travertine. Travertine is a type of limestone that is formed by mineral deposits from natural springs, so it looks kind of mottled and has random veining throughout. I was standing there with the hot water spraying on my back; when I looked, and in the veining of the tile, as plain as day, was a profile view of Mitzi's head. Not just any dog, but Mitzi. The outline of her ear, her eye, and her nose, as clear as it could be. I had never noticed it before. But now that I could see it, I couldn't unsee it. It was so obvious. And I thought, *Dang, Mama, now that's a good one!*

But wait, it gets even better. I live on Saint Simons Island in Georgia. A week or so later, I was walking with my kids in the village. We had gotten ice cream and were walking towards the pier when I saw a glint of metal on the sidewalk. At first, I thought it was a quarter but when I stopped to pick it up, it was a silver disc. It looked like a tag that might have fallen off of a dog's collar. The tag was stamped with one word. No phone number, no address, just the name—Mitzi! Unbelievable. Now, Mama was just showing off at that point. So much like her too! There was no doubt in my mind that she was sending me these signs!

> *"Every single one of us has multiple connections with the other side—those who will listen to us, who will guide us, who will help us with whatever we need."*
> —Bill Philipps

Another story that also involves a message from my mother happened fairly recently. My daughter, Maggie, was living in Savannah, Georgia, but had decided to return to college in the fall. One night in May, while out with friends, she had a short conversation with a guy sitting at the bar while she was waiting for a drink. They only spoke for a few minutes, but she felt an instant connection to him and gave him her number as she was leaving. He called her the next day and they started dating.

They really hit it off, but she was scheduled to move away at the end of July and would be moving three hours away. They were at dinner not long before she was due to leave when he told her that although he really liked her, they were just at different places in their lives, and he didn't think it was going to work out dating long distance. When she told me about their conversation the next day, I could tell she was really upset. She wasn't crying hysterically or anything like that, but I could tell she was more than just disappointed. She liked him. I mean she reeeeally liked him. I knew that, for her at least, this relationship was much more than casual; it was special.

Now I know that this kind of thing is just part of life. It happens to everybody. But you don't like to see your kid get her heart broken, and I knew that *if* they broke up, that's exactly what was getting ready to happen.

When I went to sleep that night, I had a dream that I was in my kitchen, loading the dishwasher, when my mother walked in and leaned on the counter beside me. She looked young and beautiful in the dream, not sick and frail like she did when she died. She crossed her arms and said, "You don't have to worry about Maggie. They aren't going to break up. Ben's in love with her."

And I turned to my mother and said, "How do you know? Did Maggie tell you that?"

And she said, "No, Ben told his mom, and she told me. She's a nurse." And that was the end of the dream. That's all there was to it, but it was so real and vivid.

Now, at this point, I had not even met this guy and had no clue what his mother did for a living. So, the next time I spoke to Maggie, I told her about the dream and asked her if she knew what his mother did. At the time, she didn't know either, but a few weeks later, she found out that not only was his mother a nurse, but she was a hospice nurse. A nurse who specifically deals with death and dying. And my mother was dead! How crazy is that? Needless to say, they did not break up and at the time I am writing this; they are still together.

Sometimes when I get what I call a "download" from the Universe, the voice I hear in my head will be my mother's. You know, when a thought or inspiration just pops in your head, and you know it didn't come from you. It's entirely new and out of the blue. Sometimes, I'll ask for it. I'll have something going on that I need some clarity on, and I'll just ask the Universe to give me a sign. I will literally say, "Ok, Joan, how are we going to handle this one?" And then I leave it alone and let the answers come to me.

"I think 99 times and I find nothing. I stop thinking, swim in silence, and the truth comes to me."

—Albert Einstein

Is it really her? I don't think it matters. I just know that I'm getting guidance and I receive it in a way that makes sense to me. Figure out what works for you. Most of all, heed that inner nudging. Follow your impulses. When you get the feeling or inspiration to act, do it. Even if it doesn't make sense. You have an inner compass. Trust it. Again, you have to feel for it. It's the next logical step. And then the next. And the next. Follow it.

"Have the courage to follow your heart and intuition. They somehow already know what you truly want to become. Everything else is secondary."

—Steve Jobs

"Each and every component that makes up your life experience is drawn to you by the powerful Law of Attraction's response to the thoughts you think and the story you tell about your life. Your money, and financial assets, your body's state of wellness, clarity, flexibility, size, shape, your work environment, how you're treated, work satisfaction and rewards—indeed the very happiness of your life experience in general—is all happening because of the story you tell."

ABRAHAM HICKS

You're the Author of Your Story—Edit Often

I once saw an interview of an actress who had played a stripper-prostitute in a movie. To prepare for the role, she had gone to strip clubs and talked to women who sold their bodies for money. Some were drug addicts, some had been abused, some were forced into the business by boyfriends or pimps, etc., but most of the women considered themselves to be victims. Victims of unfortunate circumstances. Until she spoke to this one woman. This particular woman had purposely chosen this profession to put herself through law school. She said she did it because the money was phenomenal. She could make in a weekend what she couldn't make in a month waitressing. She had plenty of time to study and she would be done with law school with zero debt within a year. When she was asked if she felt degraded or cheapened by the work, she said, "Absolutely not. And I'm not cheap, I'm expensive. I call the shots. I have what they want. When I walk out on that stage, they are paying to see me—paying to spend time with me. I own them, I own the room, I own the situation. I am using my assets to get what I want. It makes me feel powerful."

The actress went on to play the role in the movie from her perspective. From that "empowered" point of view. As someone who was doing the using—instead of the one who was being used.

> *"Above all, be the heroine of your life, not the victim."*
>
> —Nora Ephron

"YOU DON'T HAVE A
RIGHT TO THE CARDS YOU
BELIEVE YOU SHOULD HAVE
BEEN DEALT.

YOU HAVE AN OBLIGATION
TO PLAY THE HELL OUT
OF THE ONES YOU
ARE HOLDING."

CHERYL STRAYED

Everyone has a story. We all tell stories about who we are, where we came from, and how we ended up where we currently are. But it's the story we tell ourselves about ourselves that makes all the difference. You are either being empowered by your story or diminished by it. Does your narrative cast you as the victim, or does it enable you to take responsibility for what's within your control and allow you to move forward? Don't let the wounds of your past foreshadow your future.

Whatever your story is, it got you here, to this "right now" moment. Don't use your past consequences as an excuse to explain why you aren't where you want to be, but instead tell the story of rising above difficulties and overcoming them. Tell the story of survival, of hope, and of possibility. You get to decide what the past means for you. And you get to decide how your story plays out from here. You aren't a puppet. You're the one pulling all the strings.

Imagine yourself as a character in a movie. The movie has multiple storylines and plot twists. It has an amazing soundtrack. It's in beautiful technicolor. It's a tragedy. It's a comedy. It's unpredictable. You're the protagonist. You get to make key decisions that affect the story. How are you going to play it? It's not so much about the script you are working from, but the way you decide to play the role you've been given.

"Whatever your fate is, whatever the hell happens, you say, 'This is what I need.' It may look like a wreck, but go at it as though it were an opportunity, a challenge. If you bring love to that moment—not

discouragement—you will find the strength is there.
Any disaster that you can survive is an improvement
in your character, your stature, and your life. What
a privilege! This is when the spontaneity of your own
nature will have a chance to flow."

—Joseph Campbell

Tell a story of redemption, of happy endings, of the fact that even though you don't have all the answers, you know for sure things are working out in your favor. Replace that inner critic and negative self-talk, even if you don't yet believe it. Talk yourself into it. Edit, refine, and delete, as many times as you need to. Fine-tune your thoughts until your beliefs about your story work *for* you instead of against you.

You're the author of this saga. Decide to take the story where you want it to go. Create a new script; write a new dialogue. Everybody loves a comeback story and the game is far from over. Take the cards you are holding and play the motherfucking shit out of them.

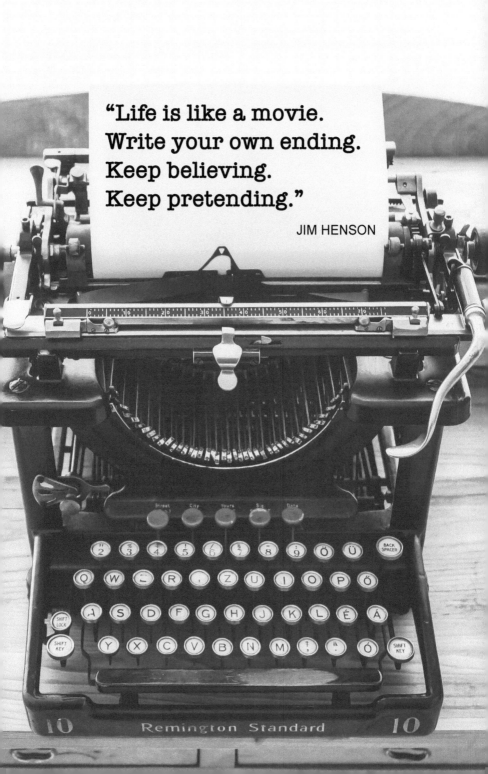

bal·ance
/ˈbaləns/

noun

1. an even distribution of weight enabling someone or something to remain upright and steady.
   "she **lost** her **balance** before falling"

2. a condition in which different elements are equal or in the correct proportions.
   "try to **keep a balance between** work and relaxation"

"I know there's a balance—

I see it when I swing past."

Balance

"Putting the Steps to Music"

We are all striving for balance. But balance is not a place you go to; balance is a skill you practice. When you ride a bike, you continuously shift your body weight and steering to return the bicycle and yourself back to the center of mass in order to remain upright. If you feel yourself start to lean too far to the left or right, you simply adjust your steering and shift your body weight to return to center. Balance is a constant adjustment of shift and movement to remain centered, to stay on the path.

> *"Life is like riding a bicycle. To keep your balance, you must keep moving."*
>
> —Albert Einstein

Navigating your vibration is like that. Since everything is vibrating energy in constant motion, there is no stopping. We are constantly in motion, either going up or down the emotional scale, swinging past center from one extreme to the other. Life doesn't stop. Though I have outlined the "rose-colored glasses perspective" in numbered steps, it is not a linear process. It's fluid and perpetual. You don't get to Step 5 and then you're done. You don't achieve balance. This is not like receiving a diploma. It's a continual, fluctuating intention. We are eternal, and there is no end point.

You don't arrive at enlightenment. You are only as conscious and aware as you can be in the "now" moment. That's why we could have a conversation, where I'm spouting off about love and compassion like I'm the Dalai Lama, and then an hour later, you could see me lose my shit in the "ten items or less" aisle at the grocery store because somebody in front of me has fifteen items in their cart.

Consciousness doesn't mean that you stay at the enlightened, high-vibrating end of the spectrum, it just means that you are aware of where you are. Sometimes you're in a state of gratitude, feeling love and kindness. And sometimes, where you are, is losing your shit and having a meltdown. You are always going to have those moments when you bump up against what you do not want.

Life is always showing you an array of choices, a plethora of people, situations, and experiences. Some things you will like and want more of and some things you won't like. But you don't go to a restaurant and feel like you have to order everything on the menu. You get to choose. You don't have to eat it all and like it. Just don't order what you don't want. Don't keep eating what you don't want and complaining about how much you don't like it. Choose.

When you see what you don't want, you understand more fully what it is that you do want. Focus on what you want. Find a view that will shift your perspective. Put on your rose-colored glasses and find some aspect of it that you can feel better about. Don't wait for the situation to improve. It can't improve as long as your focus is on what you don't want. You have to get in a

"The key to keeping your balance is knowing when you've lost it."

UNKNOWN

position to allow what you want to come to you. Think the thoughts that match what you want until you believe them. If you can align with the vibration of what you want and believe it then you can attract it.

If you're in a higher vibration then savor it. Enjoy it. Be grateful and appreciate it. Milk that good fortune, sweet love, wonderful time, delicious meal, warm, fuzzy feeling, etc., for all it's worth. Hang out there as much as you can. But it is inevitable that you will see and experience things you do not want. That's life. You're always going to be moving in one direction or the other. When you find yourself moving in the direction of a lower vibration, you will feel the discomfort of moving away from your connection to Source. It's important to experience that too. It's important to know what you do not want. You will experience shadow, but how long you decide to camp out there is up to you. How long will you tolerate it until you decide to turn it around? Balance is nothing more than the ability to get back on track when you've gotten off course.

"If you don't like where you are, MOVE. You are not a tree."

—Jim Rohn

You can never veer so far off course that you can't turn it around. No matter how far down the scale you plummet, you can always change direction. Balance is the art of deliberately navigating back up the scale, losing your footing and then finding it again, intentionally moving up the scale and catching yourself when you realize you are spiraling down. You will always be moving towards new desires, goals, and dreams because everything is in a state of becoming more. You're never stuck because you are always evolving to a new "now" moment. Every moment, it's now again. And again. And again. Every moment is a fresh start and an opportunity to choose the reality you want.

Getting back in balance is a skill you can get really good at. It just takes practice. You know you are moving towards expansion when you feel love, inspiration, hope, etc. You know that's the feeling of being in the flow, the feeling of expansion. Period. You know you are resisting expansion when you are experiencing anger, fear, guilt, etc. That's the feeling of cutting off the flow and separation from Source. Period. Choose to change direction when you need to. Adjust your perspective to move in the better-feeling direction.

That's all there is to it. You will get so good at recognizing the disconnection that it won't take much of an adjustment to realign. Just pay attention to the way you are feeling. Enjoy it when you're in the flow. Shift and modify when you're headed for the ditch. Don't make it harder than it is. Don't beat yourself up. Be easy about it. Nothing is going wrong. Trust and expect. Feel for the next step. It's like dancing.

> *"Trust the wait. Embrace the uncertainty. Enjoy the beauty of becoming. When nothing is certain, anything is possible."*
>
> —Mandy Hale

Get really good at fine-tuning your perspective in the present moment, and then all you have to do is allow the Universe to line everything up for you. There is a bigger picture. There

"PEOPLE WHO WONDER
WHETHER THE GLASS IS
HALF EMPTY OR HALF
FULL ARE MISSING THE POINT.

THE GLASS IS REFILLABLE."

UNKNOWN

are a million avenues to get the desires of your heart. You're not missing any boat or your only chance for love and happiness because there are unlimited resources and opportunities for you to be or have anything you want. Rumi said, "Live life as if everything is rigged in your favor." Because it is.

When you focus on the powerful, synchronistic parts of life, the Universe will continue to bring more of that to you. Your only job is to tune into the perfection of that. You came here to live a beautiful life. Stop trying to figure it all out and force it to happen, and just relax and trust Source to bring it to you. It is a dance of balancing your desire with your belief in the possibility of having it. When you believe that all is well and everything is working out, it is. It can't be any other way because you get what you think about.

> "Sometimes the questions are complicated and the answers are simple."
>
> —Dr. Suess

If you think the concepts presented in this book are simplistic and repetitive then you are already very perceptive. Life can be complicated. That's true. But no matter how convoluted the circumstances of life can be, the answer is always the same. And it's simple. You are going to take life as it comes and do the best you can—in the midst of whatever you are dealing with—to find some way of looking at it that makes it work for you. You are going to reach for the best-feeling thought about it that you can find. No matter what the question is, you are going to choose the perspective that brings you the most peace. You are going to choose. You. Only you.

"No matter how chaotic it is, wildflowers will still spring up in the middle of nowhere.

SHERYL CROW

Let your highest priority be to let go of the uncontrollable. Decide that no matter what is going on, your alignment to source is the most important thing. You are going to try to see the "best of it" instead of the "worst of it." You are going to be hopeful and expect the best possible outcome regardless of what is going on. Nothing ever goes wrong because it is helping you to define what you want. Trust the process even if you don't always understand it. Your only job is to "plug in." That's the only part you have to figure out how to do. The Universe supplies the power. Relax and allow yourself to move through difficulties when they arise. Believe that the Universe has everything rigged in your favor. Everything has a gestation period and is in motion. Have faith. Everything *is* working out. Later on, you will marvel at the perfect timing of the Universe, as things unfolded and lined up to give you exactly what you wanted. Even things you didn't know you wanted. You will be amazed at things coming together and falling into place in ways you couldn't have even dreamed.

If you don't get anything else from this book, I hope you are beginning to understand that it is right for you to be happy and live a wonderful life. And you alone have the ability to make that happen. Don't be so serious about it all. Lighten up. Walk the path that feels good to you. Your journey is unique to you in the sense that what works for you is not going to work for everyone else, and vice versa. Take your eyes off of them and work on you. Stop judging. Stop the struggle and the effort of pushing against. Love them because it feels good. Love yourself because you deserve it. Give yourself a break. Have fun with it. Find what inspires and uplifts you. Then do that. Do that a lot. Relax. Breathe. Pick up your feet and let the flow take you in the stream. Feel the peace of trusting and letting go. When you realize that the "feeling" of flowing with the stream was what you were searching for all along then everything else you want will come easily to you.

I love the quote from *The Wizard of Oz* when Glinda, the good witch, tells Dorothy, "You've always had the power my dear, you just had to learn it for yourself." The whole time all she had to do was to click her heels together, to go home. It had always been up to her. She didn't need help from the wicked witch *or* the wizard, to get what she wanted.

And neither do you. The key to your happiness is right there in your own pocket. Happiness is the name of the game. It's the pot of gold we are all looking for. It's real, it's attainable, and it's hiding in plain view. Put on your rose-colored glasses and decide you're going to look for the best, look for the love, look for the beautiful life that you want and deserve. Once you start looking for it, you will see...it's been right in front of you the whole time.

"WHEN I WAS FIVE YEARS OLD MY
MOTHER ALWAYS TOLD ME THAT
HAPPINESS WAS THE KEY TO LIFE.

WHEN I WENT TO SCHOOL, THEY
ASKED ME WHAT I WANTED TO BE
WHEN I GREW UP.

I WROTE DOWN HAPPY.

THEY TOLD ME I DIDN'T UNDERSTAND
THE ASSIGNMENT.

AND I TOLD THEM,
THEY DIDN'T UNDERSTAND
LIFE."

JOHN LENNON

Acknowledgements

There's not a single, original idea in this book. Just like a bird gathers grass, twigs, and items from its environment to build a nest, I have collected and scrapbooked quotes, philosophies, and the wisdom of others into a treasure trove of inspiration and guidance. Whether it's a philosopher, a scientist, a tech wizard, or a Pinterest post, the quotes and revelations I have referenced have a similar running thread. They have inspired me to reach beyond what is. And for that I am so grateful.

This book is a product of my interpretation of that wisdom and how I have applied it to my own experience. That's why I've included more than one hundred quotes in this book. I'm not making this shit up, I am only reframing the insights that I have received and hope that my current view of life might inspire someone else as they have inspired me.

To list all of the names of people who have influenced and helped me to define my perspective would be impossible. There are so many more quotes, books, people, and experiences that I didn't reference that have had equal impact but are too numerous to name. I have tried to give credit for the quotes used as accurately as I could. Most of the "Unknown" references are pulled directly off Pinterest, and to whoever posted them, I am grateful to you as well. You don't know how many of those I have used as a lifeline when I've been swimming in "Shadow" and had one too many glasses of wine.

I would like to thank Lori, Christa, Suzanne, Deanne, and Stacey for the many conversations and late-night talks that gave me the motivation to write this book in the first place. Thank you to Jeri, Janice, and Vaughn for reading the first drafts and encouraging me to pursue publication. Thank you to my babies, Maggie and Paden—by far, my greatest accomplishment and legacy. If I never do another thing, the privilege of having a part in bringing you into the world and getting a ringside seat to see the kind of generous, empathetic, and amazing humans you are is all I could ever ask for. Thank you to my mama who continues to love and guide me in unexpected ways. And to my daddy, who provided me with the last piece of the puzzle I needed to make this book a reality.

I have always loved hearing other people's stories and experiences. Biographies are my favorite. You get a window into someone's life and get to see how they did it. When you are inspired by someone else's story, you believe that if they can do it then maybe you can too. But no matter what someone has accomplished or achieved, at the very root and core of their stories, it inevitably comes down to the same thing. We all just want love, connection, and happiness. At the end of our lives, if we have been fortunate enough to catch a glimpse of that, that truly will be the only thing that mattered.

I hope that some part of this book inspires you to look for and find the love, connection, and happiness in your own roller-coaster life. That's my wish for you.

That is my wish for all of us.

Image Credits

About the Author

Robyn Barnhardt is a free-lance writer and artist. Initially, she considered writing a juicy Southern novel. Having been born and raised in the South, God knows she had the material for it. But no matter how hard she tried to change names and scenarios to protect the guilty, she decided that in the end, she would rather be on speaking terms with her friends and fami-

ly. Because that's the kind of person she is—nonconfrontational.

A self-described introvert and armchair therapist, she is likely to be found in the kitchen or back hallway during a fabulous party, discussing the meaning of life with the wait-staff. Connection over idle chit-chat is always her preference. Though not a "professional authority" on anything, she has discovered a way of looking at life that is just too good to keep to herself. So, she decided to write this book instead. Now she can hand out the book at parties and let the waitstaff get back to work.

Most days you can find her appreciating her view of life on Saint Simons Island, Georgia, with her wonderful husband and two amazing children.

RobynBarnhardt.com
Instagram @seethroughrosecoloredglasses